Embracing the Untouchables

The Story of Tommy Tillman

By Stephen Fortosis

Embracing the Untouchables
by Stephen Fortosis

Printed in the United States of America

ISBN 978-1-60477-678-2

Unless otherwise indicated, Bible quotations are taken from the King James Version.

www.xulonpress.com

Dedication

I dedicate this book to my wife, Jo Ann, and my five children: Teresa, Mitchell, Susan, David, and Lisa. My wife and I have always been a team. She loved me and stood with me through thick and thin. She is the greatest preacher's wife I've seen and the greatest Christian I know, and I love her. I have often said and still say, if she should ever leave me, I'd pack up and go with her.

Our children were always with us and assisted on the field until they grew up and married. Teresa and Lisa work together as a team in our mission office, and I don't believe this ministry could continue without their help. Mitchell answered God's call to work with the ministry in Mongolia and is doing a great job for the Lord. God gave him a wonderful Mongolian wife to work with him and support him there. Susan is married and lives in Gulf Shores, Alabama with her husband, Mark DeShazo. They are both born again Christians and they pray fervently for this ministry. David and his wife, Barbara, live in Mississippi. When Hurricane Katrina completely demolished our home and belongings, by the grace of God David and Barbara were able to survive, and they still live on the gulf coast. They're Christians and attend church.

I cannot forget my half brother, Carl Whitesel, who has always been like a full brother to me. We've always been close and he's prayed for me and supported everything I ever attempted to do for the Lord. Even at the writing of this dedication, he continues to be a great supporter of this ministry both prayerfully and financially. I'm also grateful to my sister, Barbara Trew, who has consistently been behind me one hundred percent in everything I attempted. When I first began preaching in June of 1958, she let me put up a tent on her property to conduct an old-fashioned tent revival. She didn't even charge me rent (ha). My other sister, Peggy Cooper, also assisted in so many ways. God called her to heaven last year.

Foreword

This book will be a challenge to you as a Christian to get busy for the Lord Jesus. I first met Tommy in January, 1959, as we stood in line to register at Tennessee Temple. And for as long as I have known him, Tommy Tillman has been an adventurous man. On one occasion, he hitchhiked to Birmingham, Alabama where he met a group of boys. He did not return home until he had led some of them to the Lord.

Brother Tillman started a church in Moody, Alabama. From there, he went to Mobile, Alabama and then to New Orleans, Louisiana to preach on the docks. He traveled to evangelize in Belize, Central America. Finally he went on to Thailand and finally to Mongolia.

When I first met Tommy, he was like a rose bud in God's kingdom. As he grew in the Lord, that bud opened into one of the most beautiful blooms you could imagine. But that bloom is still not fully open. I can only guess how beautiful it will be when finally in full bloom.

When I said Tommy was adventurous, I meant it, but that adventure was for the Lord and it grew out of a love for souls. This very special man is one of my best friends, and he has given his best for the Lord. Tommy could never have done this if he did not have a very special wife, Jo Ann.

May God bless all who read this book with a burden for souls.

-Dr. Albert C. Goss
Pastor, Mile Straight Baptist Church

I have known Tommy Tillman for over fifteen years and no man has impacted my life for missions as this man has. The Bible never flatters its heroes. It tells us the truth about each of them and we can see how God delights in doing what human nature thinks impossible. I believe Brother Tillman is no doubt one of God's heroes in our day.

"The burden of the Lord" is a phrase often used to describe the message of prophets in the Old Testament age. They were men of God who were aware of the circumstances about them, of the spiritual conditions, and of the need for someone to care for people. When Tommy Tillman saw the needs of lepers and orphans, like Isaiah, he said, "Here am I, send me." And the Lord did send him.

It was D.L Moody, that great soul, who set out to show the world what could be done by one man wholly devoted to the Lord. But when he came to die, he said, "The world still has yet to see what can be done by one man wholly given to the Lord."

It really is no secret what God can do. When we read of the life and works of Brother Tillman we can plainly see that God will do a great work through the spiritual dedication of one man. It is my fervent prayer that the life and ministry of this godly missionary will not only burden our hearts for those in Third World nations but also for those across the street from where we live.

—Ben Leonard
Pastor, Victory Baptist Church

Introduction

The most important thing to me is that Jesus Christ would be magnified and lifted up through this book. I want to demonstrate that God is real—how He cares for us, how He leads, and, if we follow, how He opens doors no man can open, how He gives us the right contacts, and always meets financial needs.

I love the scripture, John 3:30, "He must increase, but I must decrease." I assure you that I am nothing, absolutely nothing. I'm not a former sinner—I'm *still* a sinner and all I really deserve is hell. I wish it could be engraved on my tombstone:

> "Here lies a sinner who entered Heaven,
> But *only* by the grace of God!"

I pray from the depths of my heart that God will use this brief account to challenge Christians to be obedient to whatever the Holy Spirit instructs. I am convinced that if each of us simply obeyed the Spirit of God, we could evangelize the world. If we each reflected Christ, then Islam, Hinduism, Buddhism, and all other faiths would simply dry up and blow away.

When I was a student at Tennessee Temple in Chattanooga, Tennessee, I had a job as a janitor. I cleaned and locked down buildings after employees went home for the day. I earned little, and my wife and I owned little. But we were able to rent an apartment and buy a few groceries each week. Believe me, we learned the meaning of Hebrews 13:5: "Let your conversation be without covetousness and be content with such things as ye have, for He hath said, 'I will never leave thee, nor forsake thee.'"

In any case, a month of unexpected bills came and we did not have the fifty dollars for rent. The landlord was clamoring for the money and we knew he could evict us. We fell to our knees that evening and cried out to God. While we were praying, the phone rang and a lady told me that the Lord had laid it on her heart to offer us fifty dollars that very night. This experience opened my eyes and my heart to the true reality and compassion of God. The lady did not know our need, but God did. We have learned experientially that He is ever and always the Great Provider.

I suppose I have always been a bit of a loner in serving the Lord. I have constantly sought God and His wisdom, but I have never chased after human advice and opinion regarding how to build a ministry or do great spiritual exploits. While I was in college, I took one semester of Missions, but the theoretical programs and theories proved quite useless in the multitudes of situations and cultures to which I was called. Above all, I have tried to listen to that still, quiet voice of God speaking to my heart and spirit.

I was involved in a world missions conference near Springfield, Missouri several years ago and none of the pastors seemed interested in me, and I remember they were not interested in fellowshipping with me. I heard some of them boasting that the Baptists were the Bride of Christ and I certainly was not interested in their judgment of other Christians throughout the world. One afternoon I heard three of these pastors criticizing the idea of infiltrating Mongolia with the gospel. They were convinced that because it's a pro-Communist nation, Christians shouldn't even try to send missionaries there. Their negativity disturbed me so, I didn't even bother to tell them that our mission organization already had three flourishing churches in Mongolia.

I have never emulated or idolized so-called outstanding men of the world who have built mighty legacies. I am only interested in those whose life focus has been the Word of God and those who stand for the truth. I love what Paul wrote in Galatians 2:6: "But of these who seemed to be somewhat (whatsoever they were, maketh no matter to me—God accepteth no man's person) or they who seemed to be somewhat in conference added nothing to me."

May you discover through this book that you need nothing and no one except God:

- I have slept in cemeteries at night using tombstones for pillows.
- I have been bitten so severely by insects that the poison left me weak and dazed.

- I boarded more than one hundred Communist ships with the gospel before the fall of Soviet Communism.
- I have been in jail all night for distributing Bibles to Communist seamen.
- I slept with thirteen mangy dogs in a bamboo hut with torrents of rain all around me.
- I slept in lepers' homes.
- I enjoyed meals with lepers, eating dog meat or whatever their fare.
- I slept under bridges and in muddy alleys with lepers.

God was with me in every case and I bear the marks of Christ. That is my only boast.

—Tommy Tillman

Chapter One

On the evening of August 28, 2005, Tommy Tillman was in Rossville, Georgia closing out a missions conference. A missionary to Thailand and Mongolia, Tommy was scheduled to return to that region the following week.

After the meeting, his wife, Jo Ann, phoned and warned him not to return to their hometown that night. Within hours, Waveland, Mississippi was projected to see the eye of Hurricane Katrina. Tommy and Jo Ann planned to hide out in Tuscaloosa, Alabama until the storm was past.

On Sunday morning, August 29th, the eye of Katrina did indeed pass over Waveland. The couple waited anxiously until Tuesday morning before Tommy told his wife he was going down there alone to check out the area. He speculated that maybe a tree had fallen on the home or perhaps part of the roof was gone. When he arrived in Waveland he drove to their street and thought maybe he'd gotten confused. There was no home on the site. The structure had disappeared. In fact, the neighborhood was gone, almost the entire town was gone. It was as if a giant bulldozer had roared through wiping out everything.

Somehow Tommy had arrived in Waveland before the news media, before law enforcement, before anybody. When officials converged on the town later that day they found seven dead bodies on one home site, three dead children on another, while, nearby, bodies floated in the canals and in the Gulf of Mexico.

Near his former address, Tommy sat down on pile of rubbish and felt nauseous as he breathed in the corrupt odor of rotting garbage and dead human flesh. There was no place to go; no place to call home. He and Jo Ann had literally lost everything they owned.

At that time Tommy had been in the ministry for forty-seven years, yet Satan had never struck him as brutally and effectively as at this moment:

What kind of a God is this? You've founded orphanages and you live in a leper colony. You take homeless children and lepers off the streets, you give them a place to live and a bed to sleep on, you feed them three good meals every day, you buy all the clothes they wear and it costs them nothing. How caring can a God be who rewards you this way?

Tommy felt a surge of resentment. It was true. He had sacrificed everything to help despised outcasts. This wasn't fair. He had a good mind to call it quits; he'd stay in the United States and find a good-paying job. He and Jo Ann would earn enough to buy another home. If God wasn't going to care for them, they'd have to take care of themselves.

Suddenly an unwelcome verse popped into his head. He heard Job saying, "Though He slay me, yet will I trust Him; but I will maintain mine own ways before Him"(Job 13:15).

If that wasn't painful enough, he heard King David's voice chime in, "I have been young, and now am old; yet have I not seen the righteous forsaken nor his seed begging bread" (Psalm 37:25).

Tommy sat silently for a long time. Finally he said, "Lord, you have a reason for everything and I will not doubt your Word. I will never ask for a penny or ask for help of any kind. You are God and you own it all."

A flurry of verses rushed to his mind. "Behold the fowls of the air: they sow not, neither do they reap, nor gather into barns; yet your heavenly Father feedeth them... Are ye not much better than they? Wherefore if God so clothe the grass of the field, which today is, and tomorrow is cast into the oven, shall He not much more clothe you, O ye of little faith?" (Matthew 6:26, 30)

He heard Jesus speak again, "If ye, O Tommy, being evil, know how to give good gifts to your children, how much more shall your Father which is in heaven give good gifts to them that ask Him?" (Matthew 7:11)

He got into his car and drove all the way to Chattanooga, Tennessee where his wife waited. He had to face one of the most difficult tasks of his life. He had to look her in the eye and tell her they'd lost absolutely everything. But then he said, "Jo, I don't know how we'll make it, but we have no choice but to trust the Lord."

The next day Tommy received a letter from an unknown individual in Texas. He opened the envelope and began reading.

"Mr. Tillman, I am sending you a sum of money. This offering is not designated to your ministries in Thailand, Mongolia, or anyplace else. We know that Hurricane Katrina passed through your region. This money is so you can get relocated and settled..."

Tommy found a check for $124,000. Other churches also began sending in contributions and the Tillmans were not only able to afford a brand new home mortgage free, but were also able to buy clothing and other necessities.

Impoverished children and nomads from their mission in Mongolia somehow collected $500 to help the Tillmans recover. To these people, this was a fortune and Tommy and Jo Ann were humbled to tears.

Tommy exclaimed, "How could we not serve a Savior such as this? One who loves us and cares for every need in every crisis. He is Jehovah-Jireh: the Lord, our Provider."

Chapter Two

Tommy Tillman was born a military brat in Fort Benning, Georgia, in 1933. His family moved several times during the first fifteen years of his life. He never could get used to a place, because, as with others like him, whenever he made a few friends, his dad would be transferred to another military base.

Finally, in 1948, his father retired from the military and the Tillmans settled in Chattanooga, Tennessee. Roy Tillman eventually found a job with a company called Combustion Engineers, and Tommy spent his high school years there.

Tommy loved sports. His top sports were probably football and boxing. He boxed in Golden Gloves competitions throughout high school. The rougher the match, the better he liked it. His nose was broken in competition three times, and today it's just a soft lump of skin on his face with little bone or cartilage remaining.

He thought he was the meanest guy since Jack Dempsey and he was convinced that no one could beat him. One day he fought a boy who was reputed to be one of the finest young boxers in Tennessee. When the bell sounded, they advanced on each other and Tommy knocked him out in the first round. The next evening he beat his opponent up pretty bad too. The headline in the Sports section of the paper read: *Tiny, Terrible, Tommy Tillman does it again!*

Tommy's opponent did not show up for the third match, but officials didn't want the boy to win the Golden Gloves in his weight class by default, so they searched for a fill-in. When Tommy saw the selected boxer his confidence zoomed. The boy looked so skinny, Tommy figured maybe he'd had tuberculosis for a few years.

When they climbed into the ring and went to their corners, Tommy told his trainer, "Go get my trophy ready. I'm gonna knock this guy out and go home early. I'll take care of him real fast!"

When the bell sounded, he hurried to the center of the ring with his gloves extended. Pow! His world suddenly went black. Twenty minutes later he woke up in the dressing room. He was breathing in smelling salts and trainers were massaging his head and neck.

He mumbled, "Wha' happened? Wha' happened?"

They said, "That little, skinny old boy you fought has been boxing for fourteen years."

That's the night Tommy retired. He never fought again; He found out that there's always somebody a little bit tougher and a little bit better, and he figured his chances were better in football.

Tommy is not a massive physical specimen. If you saw him now you'd probably doubt that he played football either, but appearances can deceive. He played halfback and one thing he could do quite well was run away from people. If the quarterback gave him the ball, he wasn't about to go down easy and those monstrous tackles and linebackers chased him all over the field. He was named to Tennessee's All State team and was also on the All Southern team. He received scholarship offers from Georgia Tech, University of Georgia, the University of Miami, and a number of smaller colleges.

But somewhere between high school heroism and college dreams, Tommy met a different dream. It was a girl named Jo Ann Kelley and Cupid shot him so full of arrows he forgot all about the football scholarships.

He began walking her home from school every day lugging her schoolbooks and whatever else. Then he'd just linger at her house for dinner and throughout the evening. Finally his daddy would come by from work at midnight, pick him up and take him home.

After two or three months of this, Jo Ann's mother told his parents, "You've got to tell that boy to stop coming over here so much. It looks bad to the neighbors, him hanging out here all the time."

"I'm sorry," he told his parents, "but I just can't stay away from that girl."

So the pair decided that marriage was the only solution to their problem.

Now they've been married for over fifty years, and Tommy always tells people "I love her so much that if she ever leaves me, I'm going to be right behind her!"

However, he was pretty scrappy as a youngster, and Jo Ann had a tough streak too. They fussed some and were each just stubborn enough to make a few of those fusses into major battles. As long as he was fighting skirmishes at home, he figured it would really irk Jo Ann if he threatened to go fight a few battles overseas. He said, "I'll take care of you. You want to get rid of me? I'll go join the Army."

Much to his surprise, she said, "Go ahead, I dare you!"

The experience taught Tommy to be more careful about challenging his wife. The Army stuck him in the infantry and carted him off to Korea. He began sending his wife a letter every day:

"Honey, sweetheart, baby doll, can you get me out of this? I'm sorry—I'll never argue with you again."

She'd reply, "You stay over there, buster! You asked for it. Now you have to stay out your commission."

So Tommy fought in Korea for two years and when he returned he wasn't so interested in fussing with his wife anymore.

Tommy arrived back in the States in 1956, and found a job with L & N Railroad in Chattanooga. At this point in his life, it had been four years since he'd attended a church. He walked into a barber shop one afternoon and waited for his turn. There was absolutely nothing to read in that place except a gospel tract. His parents had told him very little about the Bible and he didn't even know what a gospel tract was. He picked up that little piece of paper and what he read pierced him right through the heart. It told him he was a sinner and needed forgiveness desperately. The Holy Spirit began convicting his spirit, and this gentle prodding would continue for over a year.

To assuage the inner voice, he discussed plans with Jo Ann for attending church. But they discussed it like they were planning a vacation. They'd look a few months ahead and claim that if nothing intervened, they would attend church then. But that Devil followed them around and, sometimes even as they climbed the steps of a church they'd be irate or distracted about something.

They attended church sporadically and friends would occasionally drag Tommy with them and coax him up to the altar. However, he wasn't ready to make a genuine commitment to Christ. And he told Jo Ann that if God ever did save him, he was going to keep quiet about it because it was a private matter.

Then one evening in early 1958 Tommy and Jo Ann showed up at a church, and he sat as far back as possible—back where the shadows hid him from the pastor's gaze. As the sermon progressed he glanced at his wife accusingly: "You called that preacher and told him about me, didn't you?"

He seemed to know every one of Tommy's secret sins; it was as if he was reciting his life story. When the invitation came, the young man walked forward and fell to his knees. Someone came and read the Bible to him and prayed. He invited Christ into his life that night and was born again.

He immediately rushed home and began calling aunts, uncles, nieces, nephews, friends and neighbors to tell them what Jesus had done for him. Seven days later, he began proclaiming the message.

First, Tommy went out and bought a massive Bible. He found the largest Bible in Chattanooga, figuring the bigger the Bible one owns, the closer he is to God. He hauled that Bible to church every Sunday and pledged, "I'm going to do every single thing the Bible says."

Tommy spread the word that he liked to preach and a small church invited him to fill their pulpit on a Sunday. The church seemed to like preachers who hollered a lot, so Tommy stood up and preached for all he was worth for an hour and a half. He preached from Genesis to Revelation, and added any stories or illustrations he'd heard.

The next Sunday, the church invited him back and Tommy stood and preached for about two minutes before he fizzled out. He had preached everything he knew the week before.

Tommy was such a beginner in the faith that he thought all religions and denominations were basically the same, just with different names. He saw an ad announcing a big religious convention in the area baseball stadium, and he thought *What a great idea! I'll go get some more teaching from the Bible.*

When he first arrived at the stadium, he noticed that he was one of the few carrying a Bible. But he went ahead and found a good seat where he could see and hear the speakers well.

As the sermons progressed, a lot of what Tommy was hearing wasn't exactly the way his Sunday school teacher had taught it. A speaker was claiming that only 144,000 would make it to Heaven. The only other place in the Bible where he recalled hearing about this number was the 144,000 Jewish witnesses who'd proclaim God's Word during the last days. These people seemed to be saying that vast numbers would simply be annihilated.

Tommy began asking questions of those around him: "If there's no everlasting punishment for anyone, what does it mean in Matthew when Jesus says, 'And these shall go away into everlasting punishment but the righteous into life eternal'?"

People stared at him and muttered to one another.

Tommy continued, "And if there's no torment in hell, what does Revelation 14:11 mean when it says, 'And the smoke of their torment ascendeth up forever and ever and they have no rest day or night'?"

By this time Tommy was getting warmed up and his voice became louder and louder. Finally an elderly man came over to him, told him he was causing a disturbance, and asked if he was a Jehovah's Witness. When Tommy said no, he said, "If you'll give me your name and address, I'll send you all the answers you're seeking."

Forty-seven years later, Tommy has still not received the answers.

Chapter Three

Tommy decided he needed more training in this whole Bible thing and enrolled in Tennessee Temple University in December, 1959. He read in Matthew where Jesus says, "Go ye into all the world and preach the gospel to every creature…"

Taking that command very literally, he began preaching on the streets of Chattanooga. Then during the summers he began traveling cross-country, preaching everywhere he went. A few folks responded but most looked at him like he was several cards short of a full deck. He had a lot to learn.

However, God did bless Tommy with some valuable evangelizing experience. At one point, he was canvassing homes in eastern North Carolina, asking each occupant if they knew Jesus.

He found a woman out hoeing her vegetable garden. When he asked if she knew she was saved and going to Heaven, she said, "Yes, I sure do."

Tommy said, "Maam, how is it that you know that?"

"Well, I was planting seeds in my garden and all at once I felt good all over and I started ashoutin'. Chills ran up and down my spine and I was so excited I actually passed out. When I woke up sometime later, I was saved. Nobody could feel that way without being saved."

"But have you been saved the way the Bible says?"

She leaned on her hoe. "Which way's that?"

They walked over to her front porch, sat down on her steps, and Tommy presented the complete plan of salvation. Then he asked if she'd like to repent and invite Christ into her life.

She said, "I sure will do that. I'll do it right now."

After her prayer, her eyes lit up and she began to rejoice and thank God.

Tommy asked her how she knew she was born again and she said, "I did what that there Bible says, and the Bible does not lie."

He rose to leave but she shouted through the screen door, "John, come on out here to the porch right now."

Her husband appeared and she said, "Tell him what you just told me."

Tommy explained the gospel again, and the man prayed to receive Christ. Tommy was walking out to the street when the woman hollered to her son in the barn to come quick.

He explained the gospel to young Jimmy, and he was saved on the spot too. Tommy left that home with three excited family members embracing and weeping with joy.

In 1962, while still attending college, he took a pastorate at the Hill Top Baptist church in the small town of Ooltewah, Tennessee. He was a young rooster for God, proud of his knowledge and wishing to crow about it every chance he got. He had not yet learned very much about humility, wisdom, and tact. Thus, Tommy succeeded in taking a church with 85 members and ending up with somewhere around 15 in only one year. He learned the hard way that pastoring is not just preaching and setting people straight. It is working side by side with them, loving them, and living ordinary life with them day in and day out.

Anyway, after he'd done some damage, hurt some people, and run some folks off, he resigned and accepted a youth pastorate at Calvary Baptist Church in Knoxville, Tennessee. There he began learning how to do grass roots ministry from the ground, up. Besides working with the teens, he also headed up the church bus ministry.

In 1965, Tommy and Jo Ann accepted a call to the Forrest Hills Baptist Church in Atlanta. There, Tommy helped build the church bus routes with Pastor Curtis Hutson, a man who would later serve as managing editor of the Sword of the Lord newspaper.

Back when attending Tennessee Temple, Tommy had gone to Mexico City with a senior who knew the area, and he served there for four weeks. He'd enjoyed that short-term mission, so he told his wife this might be just the ticket for them.

In 1966, they began ministering at the U.S.-Mexican border, with frequent forays into various Mexican cities. But after serving in Mexico for three very long years, he told Jo Ann, "I'm so tired of this. It feels like I'm slamming my head against a wall every single day. I don't think God wants us to live this way—facing constant opposition, fighting with Catholics, enduring threats..." He said, "Let's go back to America, I'll just get an ordinary job somewhere and we'll find a fine conservative church to attend."

He didn't think at this point that God could use him as a preacher or a missionary. In fact, he told Jo Ann, "I'm just not going to preach anymore. Maybe I've missed my calling."

But God wasn't done with him. God got his attention in a way he couldn't deny. His health began to fail. Tommy felt sick all the time and began to pass blood. His doctor couldn't find a cause so he was admitted into a hospital for some tests.

The first morning in the hospital, they took him down to the X-ray room and injected a dye that would indicate any problems with the kidneys. Within minutes, Tommy's entire body was burning—as if flames were enveloping his insides.

He wanted to scream *Doctor, I need help. I'm burning up!*

But he could not speak. His tongue was paralyzed. He tried to lift his arm and motion to the staff but couldn't move an inch.

Suddenly the doctor whirled and gave him a hard look. He turned to the nurse, "Go get another doctor. He's reacting to the dye."

The nurse fled the room and Tommy lay there with his heart crashing through his chest: Boom,

boom, boom! All at once, he felt a terrible thud in his chest and began to sink into a very long, dark tunnel. Then he saw a light brighter than anything on earth, and he heard the words in his mind, "I am the vine, ye are the branches. If a man abide not in me, he is cast forth as a branch and is withered..."

When he regained consciousness, his eyes fluttered open, and he glimpsed three doctors hovering over him. They said, "Boy, we almost lost you. Your heart stopped beating for two and a half minutes..."

He knew without a doubt that God had given him one of those wake up calls.

In any case, the doctors isolated a prostate problem, and when Tommy recovered and his feet hit the floor, he got busy again in God's work and he hasn't slowed down since.

In 1971, Tommy and Jo Ann moved to Leeds, Alabama where they rented an old store building, swept and scrubbed it, painted the walls, had some carpet installed and began knocking on doors. On the first Sunday, they were thrilled when fifty-three people showed up. The first year, one hundred and thirty five joined the church. Tommy pastored that church for five years, and today it has grown into a large and thriving work.

In 1977, Tommy sensed a call from God to New Orleans where he began developing a ministry to seamen. He and Jo Ann rented an old building on Magazine Street in New Orleans and made it their mission headquarters. They named the ministry

Harbor Evangelism International, a name that would stick in spite of the fact that the ministries would spread far, far beyond the docks of New Orleans.

It was during this move that a minor incident taught Tommy a lesson in Christian love. Every time Tommy and Jo Ann moved, his job was always hanging their pictures and paintings on the walls—with his wife's approval, of course.

So one afternoon he picked up a nail between forefinger and thumb and placed it on the wall.

Jo Ann said, "To the right…"

"Yes, dear."

"Move it up a few inches."

"Yes, dear."

"That's where I want it. Hit it," she said.

Tommy swung back the hammer and BAM he hit the nail, but it was the wrong nail—he got his thumb. He saw blood building behind his thumb nail and he could feel that awful throbbing: boomp, boomp, boomp! The thumb swelled up like a big purple plum, and Tommy danced the Bebop Boo, the Buckaloo, the Two-Step, the Applejack, the Jitterbug, and the Waltz. He danced through every room in the house and then out into the front yard—screaming and hollering.

But as the pain blurred into a hard, dull ache, Tommy realized that when his finger got smashed, his body didn't say, "Hey, buddy, we're going to have to get rid of you; you're giving us too much pain and suffering. Remove yourself from this body; we refuse to fellowship with you anymore!"

On the contrary, the other hand grabbed that thumb oh so gently and kissed it, and held it close to the chest. And after about an hour, the thumb was feeling better, back in happy fellowship with the body.

After a few hours, Jo Ann said, "Honey doll, you think we can get that picture up now?"

"What's with this 'we' stuff?" said Tommy.

"Well, I know you got hurt, but we can work together on this."

"Okay, dear, here we go."

Now he placed the nail between two fingers, giving his poor thumb a rest. Then he pulled the hammer back and she said, "A little to the right and up."

"Yes, dear."

"Hit it."

But instead of slamming it, all Jo Ann heard was a peck, peck, peck against that nail. Tommy had learned his lesson.

As Tommy thought about it, he saw a powerful lesson in the experience. Through the years he had seen many ugly church divisions, and dissension in other ministries as well. He knew that most of these clashes ended sadly or even disastrously. People gave way to bitterness and anger, fussing and tearing each other down. And if a brother or sister fell into some sin, Christians often "shot their own wounded." Tommy realized the importance of loving that one, offering restoration, and bringing him or her back into fellowship the way he'd brought his thumb "back into fellowship" with the body.

Tommy and Jo Ann began inviting seamen to come and relax in their comfortable center, and among those to whom they ministered were Communist sailors from Russian ships.

This was before the fall of Communism in the Soviet Union, which makes it even more amazing that, in time, Tommy was able to distribute Bibles on over one hundred Russian ships. He boarded many ships in a way that could only have been engineered by God Himself.

One week a Russian ship came to pick up farm tractors. A large group of longshoremen gathered to help load the tractors. Tommy began mingling with them and soon he was talking away as if he knew them. As they boarded the ship, Tommy just followed them— the Russians thought he was a longshoreman and the longshoremen thought he was a Russian. He left many gospel tracts on the ship that day.

One night as he tried to board a Russian ship, several blocked his way. One said, "You cannot come on this ship. This is our territory and the captain doesn't want you here."

Tommy stood there with all his Russian-language Bibles and gospel tracts, and prayed silently. *Dear God, you've opened the door for me to board these ships before, and you haven't let me down yet. Please make a way.*

He turned around and left the ship. As he walked away he glanced up at the Greater New Orleans Bridge. He knew that thousands and thousands of cars pass over that bridge every day. There are signs on the bridge that read: "In case of a flat, continue driving until you are off the bridge." With all that traffic, even a delay of minutes can cause a massive back-up. Suddenly an idea hatched in his head. He entered the highway, moving toward the bridge. When he reached the center of the bridge, he stopped his car and hopped out. People immediately began yelling and honking. One man shouted, "What are you going to do, you nut, jump?"

Tommy grabbed that big bundle of Bibles and tossed it over the railing. It seemed as if an angel guided the bundle that day because partway down it struck a sharp edge, the twine broke, and that entire Russian ship was suddenly covered with gospel tracts and Bibles. Sailors scrambled for the literature. He had succeeded in spite of them.

More and more Soviet ships began denying him entrance as they realized he carried Bibles. So he sat down to regroup and pray about what to do. Suddenly he recalled that many ships in port will allow civilians on board if they only wish to fish off the bow or stern. He went home and donned his big bib overalls, collected his rod and reel, put on his straw hat, and stowed Bibles and tracts in his many pockets. When he returned to Russian ships, they allowed him on board. He'd fish until the sun went down. Then he'd infiltrate the ship, distributing the materials.

When one does this type of ministry for years, word begins getting around. One day Tommy boarded a Russian ship and they grabbed him. Seamen took him below decks.

"Now you're in big trouble," they said. "Who gave you the authority to board. We might be docked in America, but you're on our territory now. No one gets off this ship unless we allow them."

Tommy was scared. He knew that they could literally make him disappear, and no one would ever find his body. At this awful moment, what should burst upon his mind but the story of Peter Rabbit, Brer Fox, and Brer Bear. In the story the young rabbit is captured by the fox and bear and Peter says, "You can do anything you want with me, but please don't throw me into the briar patch."

He covered his face. I'm losing my mind. These seamen are threatening my life and I'm thinking about kids' stories. I've finally fallen over the edge.

Then something clicked in his mind. Peter Rabbit pled with his captors *not* to do what he really desired. He could make the seamen desperate to get him out of their hair.

"I'll tell you why I boarded this ship," he proclaimed. "You caught me before I could stow away. I planned to sail to Russia with you and hand out these Bibles on the streets of Moscow."

They stared at one another wide-eyed. "This man is insane," they muttered. "He's completely cracked up."

They took him by the arms, hurried him to the deck of the ship and pushed him down the dock and away. "Don't come back here," they called. "You're a crazy man."

There were times when Tommy went to extremes in his quest to spread the Word. One night he placed four hundred Bibles on a ship and the captain became so incensed that he called in the FBI. The captain contacted them without Tommy's knowledge and claimed that he headed up a smuggling operation. The Russian wanted something done about it.

The FBI staked out the dock and arrested him as he departed from the ship. They called the Harbor Police who arrested him and delivered him to jail. Stewing in a jail cell at 3:00 a.m., Tommy prayed, "Dear God, if I'm in your will, what am I doing in this jail tonight?"

The next morning the judge ushered him into his chambers. He said, "Your case is on the docket for today. I know what you were doing, and, quite honestly, I'm sympathetic to your cause. But there are some lawyers who can't wait to attack you and make an example out of you. They will do all they can to crush you. This really caused an uproar—those Russians finding all this contraband on their ship."

Tommy said, "Your honor, what am I being charged with?"

"Criminal trespassing."

He shook his head vigorously. "I did not criminally trespass. Every time I've been asked to vacate a ship, I have done so willingly."

"But were you on the ship?"

"Well, yes."

"Then I must charge you. But I'll tell you what, I'm going to suspend the sentence." He stood. "Just stay away from those ships."

Tommy stood before the judge in the courtroom: "Do you plead guilty to the charge of boarding the Russian ship?"

He said, "Judge, I did not criminally trespass."

The judge's jaw tightened. "Were you on the ship?"

"Yes sir, I was on board. I'd have left if they'd just asked nicely."

"Since you were on the ship, I'm going to charge you with trespass. I am sentencing you to six months suspended sentence. Don't even think of going back to the waterfront for six months."

But God's laws are greater than human laws. The next day he was again trying to board Communist ships. But now he was black-balled. There had even been newspaper articles about him. When he walked up gangplanks now, the first thing seamen said was, "What is your name?"

Their antennae were up. But Tommy figured, what's wrong with a half-truth to further the kingdom of God? It isn't lying. His middle name was Leroy so that's how he introduced himself now.

Finally the Louisiana Senator's office telephoned and said, "We are aware of what you're doing. If you're going to attempt giving out Bibles on these ships, we advise you to constantly move from port to port. That way, you'll be gone before anyone can arrest you."

Chapter Four

Tommy continued working among the seamen, but then he heard about some open doors in Belize, Central America. He traveled to Belize and hitched a ride on a banana truck to Punta Gorda, the area where the Maya Indians lived. This was on a Friday.

When Tommy reached the village, the Mayas would have nothing to do with him. They wouldn't even allow him to enter their village. He went to hitch a ride back to Belize but found no vehicles were headed in that direction until sometime Monday.

Friday night he found a cemetery to sleep in. In order to avoid at least some of the insect onslaught, he slept on a concrete slab. He haunted the cemetery all weekend and when he returned to Belize City on Monday, his whole body was one swollen mass of insect bites. He found a motel with four rooms and a communal shower, but he couldn't afford to be picky. He collapsed on the bed and slept for twenty hours straight. When he awoke, he went to take a shower and just when he was all soaped up, the water cut off.

"Water shortage," shouted the motel manager. "We must shut water off from five p.m. to eight a.m." He didn't even seem sorry about it.

Tommy wiped as much soap off his body as he could and went for another 24 hours with a sticky body and itchy sores.

Of course, Tommy wasn't ready to give up on the Mayan ministry. He and a partner flew down to Belize, and as they bought supplies, suddenly they saw a limousine approach and stop not twenty feet away. A chauffeur climbed out and went around to open the door. Out stepped a Korean woman dressed immaculately. She wore rings, bracelets, and necklaces that must have been worth thousands.

"What are you doing here?" she asked.

Tommy wanted to ask her the same question but he explained that he was searching for the Maya Indian tribe.

"Who is this tribe you speak of?"

As the people were described to her, the woman stood spellbound. She could not stop asking questions about the tribe and why Tommy and his partner were going to them. Finally she stepped back into the limo and they drove away. Tommy expected never to see her again.

Tommy and his friend drove deep into the jungles, crossing three sturdy rope bridges in the process. Then it began to rain and the rain became a deluge. When they reached a fourth bridge the water level was too high and rushing too fast to cross it. They turned around to return to Belize City, but the bridge behind them was also flooded. They sat alone in the pick-up truck for three days and nights. They rationed a few crackers they had brought and drank lukewarm Coke. Then the food was gone.

Suddenly an old man appeared out of the jungle. It was Sho, chief of the Mayas. "We watch you for three days," he said. "You in trouble; come to my village with me."

When they reached the site, they were surrounded by approximately one hundred villagers. The chief said, "You stay in bamboo house until the river goes down and you can return to your city."

Chief Sho's house had two rooms and housed thirteen dogs. The stench was almost overpowering. After a few hours in there, Tommy said, "I've got to go outside. I can't stand this."

He went outside and sat in the hard rain until he was waterlogged. Back and forth he went, not sure which place was worse.

The chief returned and said, "We know you must be hungry and you also need some coffee. I bring you a nice, hot cup of coffee."

Wow, that sounded good!

A little later he returned with two bowls of coffee. Tommy took a sip, then almost spilled the liquid all over himself. A huge roach was swimming around in the coffee.

Tommy sputtered, "Do I have to drink this, Lord?"

The Holy Spirit said, "Well, you've been dying of thirst. Here is your answer."

"Lord, bless this coffee," whispered Tommy. He flipped the roach onto the ground and gulped the liquid.

The chief said, "We feed you now. Feed you good food."

Tommy was ravenous. At least the chief understood their needs.

Soon, in he marched with a large platter of scrambled eggs.

When Tommy saw the eggs, his stomach went boompety, boomp, boomp. Mixed liberally in the eggs he glimpsed quite a variety of hairs.

"Please, Lord," he prayed, "my stomach's turning somersaults. Do we have to eat this?"

The verse flashed across his mind, "Whatsoever is set before you, eat, asking no questions…"

He grinned to himself. The scriptural context was different, but it was interesting that this popped into his mind.

"Lord, bless these eggs and don't let us lose them prematurely," he murmured, and began eating.

They spent the night with the dogs, and in the morning Chief Sho appeared. "You can come stay with us anytime," he said. "You stayed in bamboo house and did not think you were superior to us."

Now Tommy felt he'd earned the right to tell the chief about Jesus. But the chief was quite firm: "Listen to me, we are Catholics. We will never change our faith. However, you came down here, you ate with us, stayed with us—you can come to preach anytime you want. We are your friends but don't think we will ever change our religion."

Tommy returned to New Orleans and a few months passed. Then in December, 1979, a torn, mud-spattered piece of mail arrived from Belize. It contained a brief, cryptic note from Chief Sho in his language: *"Please come back to our village. You have shown you are one with our people and we want to hear more of your words."*

Tommy began periodically visiting the village and speaking of Christ through an interpreter. One night after midnight, Chief Sho woke him up.

"Mister Tillman, I think something is wrong with me."

Tommy rubbed the sleep from his eyes. "What is it?"

"I cannot rest," he said. "My heart will not let me sleep. Maybe you can help me."

"Mr. Sho, I believe you need to be born again."

"Can you explain to me?"

Tommy spent about an hour explaining scripture to Chief Sho and he won the chief to the Lord that night. The next day they spoke about what being a Christian really means and the chief learned about baptism.

That night well after 11:00 p.m. he woke Tommy again.

"What do you need, Chief?"

"You said Bible teaches must be baptized. I know I am already born again, but I need baptism to be obedient servant."

"That's right...but do we have to do it now?" Tommy knew that dangerous snakes swam that river.

Chief nodded. "And before we go, I will wake everyone in village." He began hurrying from hut to hut. "Wake up! Wake up! A great thing happens tonight. Come to the river."

They stumbled to the river with flashlights and simple lanterns. Tommy and Chief Sho went into the water up to their waists. Chief looked back at all those Maya Indians on the banks and said, "Now you know I have been your leader and I have always done what I thought was best for village. Because this man brought gospel to us, I found out that going to Heaven is through the Lord Jesus Christ, not through the Church." He paused to let the words sink in. "I am leaving Catholic Church, and I am trusting Christ for salvation. Now I am ready to be baptized."

He turned solemnly to Tommy. "All right, Mr. Tillman, baptize me now."

It was after midnight when the chief went under that water in the name of the Father, Son, and Holy Spirit. In the days to follow, the entire village followed their leader's example and were born again.

Tommy eventually brought Chief Sho to the United States and invited him to give his testimony in many churches. The pair traveled together and sometimes stayed in hotels overnight. Tommy was surprised to find that Chief would not sleep in beds. Apparently, he was more comfortable on the floor. That was fine, but the one thing that disappointed Tommy a little is that he wouldn't take baths either.

Night after night in a hotel room with Chief became a bit of an odoriferous challenge.

Over the months, Tommy and his partner taught the Chief all they could about pastoring a church. When he returned to his people, the Catholics came down wanting to know why the priest wasn't welcome in the village anymore.

When the villagers heard Catholic officials were on their way, they hid Tommy in the little bamboo house. "Don't you come out," they said. "Stay in there until trouble is over."

"What trouble are you talking about?"

"You just stay in there and be quiet."

Soon Tommy heard loud voices outside. A priest asked, "Where is this man, Tillman? He's the one who came down here and destroyed the village."

Chief Sho and the men of the village answered, "If you touch this man, you will start a war. He came down to us and told us the truth."

The Chief and his men eventually tore down the Catholic church building. They said, "We are not trusting the church to take us to Heaven. We trust in Jesus only."

Tommy began traveling through the jungles winning people to Christ and building churches throughout the Belize region. Sometimes he took friends with him. Once, a Texas friend named Charles O'Neal wanted to visit the Mayas. They rented a vehicle in Belize City and drove to Punta Gorda where the Mayas lived. A storm hit and it was raining so hard they could barely see the dirt road ahead. They didn't want to fall off an overhang or get stuck in a ditch so they stopped at an old house and woke the occupants. Tommy asked if they could sleep on their porch or even under their home, but the residents said they had a spare room. When the pair pulled back the covers in the guest room, hundreds of bedbugs squirmed for cover. Needless to say, they spent the night on the floor.

The most remarkable thing happened a year or two later. Tommy went down to check on the mission work in Belize and visited the Mayas. As he walked into the village, a Korean woman stepped out of a hut wearing the same garb as the Indians. Tommy did a second take. Yes, it was really her — the wealthy woman who had stepped out of the chauffeured automobile long before and had seemed so fascinated regarding the Mayas. She had become a Christian and dedicated herself to living among them and serving them.

During this period, Tommy began hearing about an almost completely neglected population evangelistically. In many countries, lepers were not just considered low class, they were considered the "untouchables." As Tommy's focus began to shift, God raised up a man from Mississippi to take over the work in Belize. This man eventually founded a Bible college and today native pastors are being trained and sent out from that center.

At the Port of New Orleans in 1983, Tommy met a South Korean Christian. The man invited him to come to South Korea and preach in his church.

On one of the trips, Tommy met another individual who asked him to preach in his village, but he didn't explain just what sort of village it was.

From Pusan, they led him far back through the mountains. The weather was cold—somewhere below 20 degrees. The party finally reached the village gate at about midnight. Through the darkness, Tommy saw figures scuffling down the trail to the gate—individuals on homemade crutches, some missing arms, others blind or with misshapen faces, all moving slowly, painstakingly, guiding one another toward the gate.

When they reached the gate, one asked through an interpreter: "Are you the one who's come to preach to us?"

Tommy nodded and the gate slowly scraped open.

"We have been waiting for you," they said. "We want you to preach the Bible to us."

They took Tommy to a shanty and fed him; then they escorted him to a small meeting place. As he entered, he heard the roomful of lepers singing in their language: "What a friend we have in Jesus, All our sins and griefs to bear, What a privilege to carry everything to God in prayer…"

Tommy looked around and saw lepers with ravaged faces and only nubs where arms and legs should have been. They'd wrapped thin blankets around their decaying bodies. He was moved as he heard them singing the song from their hearts. Tommy had been told it was considered impolite to wear shoes indoors, so as he entered the structure, he removed his shoes. He walked to the front of the chapel and a leper crawled over to him.

"We know that you are not used to our climate," he said, "and your feet will freeze so I'm going to massage them."

As temperatures dipped down below zero, he rubbed Tommy's feet and kept massaging them throughout the whole evening of preaching. Tommy could hardly preach for weeping about this leper guarding him from frostbite.

At 2:00 a.m. they ushered him to a 9'x 9' room where he lay down on a pallet. About two and a half hours later, he heard a knock at the door. Who in the world would be waking him after only a few hours of sleep? Tommy opened the door and a leper said, "We want you to come now and preach to us some more."

"But it's four thirty in the morning!"

"None of us could sleep. We want you to come and preach to us again and they sent me to get you."

Tommy dressed and got back down to the chapel at 5:00 a.m. Every one of those lepers was back in there.

He breathed a prayer. "Dear God, these people barely let me sleep at all. I can't be a missionary to people like this."

They held a service until daybreak, yet the people still didn't want to leave. They said, "Preach to us some more!"

So he preached on until he'd preached almost every sermon he could recall. When he finally ran out of gas, the impoverished lepers took an offering and gave him $25.00, which was for them a small fortune. He only took the offering because he'd been taught that if he refused it, he may rob the givers of a greater blessing from God.

As the hours passed, God began moving in Tommy's heart. By the time he left the village he was able to pray: "Lord, I don't want to do anything simply out of sympathy or pity, but if you want me to be a missionary to people like this, please give me a definite calling."

In October, 1983, someone took him out to Schruch-do: Leper Island, which is thirty miles out in the Yellow Sea. Twenty four hundred lepers lived on this island. They lived within view of a crematorium where they watched the smoke of friends and relatives being burned to ash.

Tommy learned that the people worship five gods and keep them locked in an enclosure so they cannot escape. Word began to spread that somebody had come to tell them about a God who loved them. That first evening Tommy watched over 1500 lepers crawling on their elbows and knees along the road and up the side of the hill to the meeting place.

The theme of Tommy's first message was: We don't need exterior decoration; we need interior regeneration. He preached about Christ's death, the blood that washes away all sin. He told them of the need for repentance and new birth. And, my how their faces lighted up when he told them that in Heaven believers will receive a glorified new body. Tommy heard the sound of weeping in the crowd.

When he gave the invitation, a few hundred lepers crawled on their knees to the front to receive Jesus. That's when he told God, "These fields are obviously white for harvest. If these people are so desperate they will crawl to Christ, I give you my heart now to devote my life to them."

Later that same day Tommy was invited to preach in a leper prison. Leprous criminals were kept in a separate prison lest other prisoners contract the disease. When the prisoners were invited to accept Christ, eleven stepped forward, including one prison guard.

High in the mountains, Tommy also found a leper colony consisting of only twenty-five small shelters built solely with mud and grass. He was the first white man they had ever seen. Tommy was able to procure five hundred dollars worth of cassette tape players with Bible recordings in the Korean language. These were left especially for the seven hundred blind lepers so they could learn.

Two hundred miles away from the leper colonies Tommy found an orphanage which housed the children of lepers who are taken at birth and will never see their parents alive. He found them eating, sleeping, and living like the lowest dogs, and he contributed $1000 to buy clothing, food, and Bibles for the children.

Chapter Five

Tommy noticed lepers begging by the side of roads and hidden in enclaves away from those who despise them. However, he still had more to learn about earning their respect and acceptance. Individual lepers begging in the cities paid him little attention at all. But one afternoon he had an epiphany that changed his life and opened the door even wider for ministry among these people.

He was walking down a bustling city street and saw a street beggar with leprosy. He walked over to him and said through an interpreter, "Son, let me tell you about somebody that loves you."

The man would not even look at Tommy. "I know who you want to tell about. His name is Jesus and I do not want to hear about this person anymore."

"You don't want to hear about Jesus?" Tommy said. "Don't you know he loves you and died for you?"

"I have heard that over and over from you Christians," he spit out. "To me, it is just hot air coming out of your mouths."

"What do you mean?"

"I have been on this corner for two years begging you Christians to walk down the street into my home, but you just throw a few coins at me."

"What's wrong with trying to help you?"

"I would like to see some of this love from God you talk about. No Christian has ever spent the night in my home. No one has ever sat down and shared a meal with me. Yet you say that you love me."

God convicted Tommy at that moment. He thought he was winning the man's heart by giving him money, but before the leper would take the gospel seriously, he needed to see that Tommy was willing to spend time with him, dine with him, and sleep in his home. Most people recoiled and couldn't stand his disfigurement. But all he wanted was to be allowed to serve. Tommy went home with the leper that evening and slept on a pallet with him on the bare floor.

The next morning the leper's daughter made some breakfast. Tommy and his host sat down to eat, and with his nubby hand, the leper took some food from his plate and placed it on Tommy's. He said, "This tastes so good. Try it and tell me if you like it. Go ahead."

Tommy froze. He couldn't do it. He could not reach out and eat that food that a leper had just touched. Silently, he cried out, "God, I spent the night in this home. I've gone this far, but I've frozen up. Can you help me eat this food? I just can't do it!"

He felt a warmth, a peace from God fill him, and he reached out and took a bite of the food, then another.

Tears began falling from the leper's eyes. "Mister, this is what I have always been waiting for. Now, tell me about Jesus."

The old leper was born again at the breakfast table.

A week later, Tommy went to preach in a village about twenty miles away. He rose, stood at the pulpit and glanced outside. There stood his leper friend. The man waved a stump and said, "Preacher, they won't let me come in, but I will go anywhere to hear you. You showed me God's love; you didn't just tell me about it."

The next week, he spoke in another church, and there sat that leper in the dusty yard.

"Preacher, I'm still following. I'll go anywhere to hear you preach. If I can be there, you know I won't miss it."

Tommy received a letter from his daughter some years later while he was on furlough. She wrote, "Brother Tommy, daddy has died now and gone to Heaven. But I thank God that someone came and showed him God's love instead of just telling him about it."

At the churches in which Tommy preached during that furlough, he stated his belief that the great cry of the world today is: *Show us God's love.*

He said, "I believe some of the charismatics' doctrine is in error, but do you know why many of their churches are growing by leaps and bounds? It is because when a person attends their churches, he or she is loved. These folks often demonstrate God's love in daily, practical ways.

"I can jump on the Baptists," Tommy said, "because I'm an ordained Baptist minister. I'll be a Baptist until my memory goes and they stick me in some institution. I'm with the Baptists like they're my own family. If my kids do something wrong, I'll spank them, but I don't want anyone else doing that. And one area in which we Baptists tend to fail is showing God's love unconditionally.

"Let's not wait for people to come to us. Let's not wait for Thanksgiving or Christmas to give out baskets. Find people who are needy and go spend the evening with them. Go locate the sickest person you can find and sit at that person's bedside. Tell people that you love them. Do things for them; buy things for them. Then tell them about Jesus Christ."

Referring to his biblical education, Tommy declared, "I studied Greek, Hebrew, and complex theological doctrines and philosophies, but none of that has been nearly as helpful in my ministry as this simple truth of loving people from the heart with God's compassion and proving that love whenever possible."

A full time co-worker emerged in late 1983 to work among the Korean leper population. His name was Ye-Young Yang, nicknamed Barnabas Yang. He not only began preaching the gospel to lepers but also initiated a training center for ministers to the 120 leper colonies in Korea at that time.

From the beginning, Tommy's ministry was not a generic, anonymous counting of souls or an arrogant declaration of a "Westernized" gospel. It was a deeply caring and personal lifestyle of servanthood. The bodies of most of the lepers at this time were too deteriorated from neglect to benefit much from surgery, but Tommy found one little island girl in the Yellow Sea with a hare-lip and cleft palate. He determined that this infant would be helped. The lip was repaired, the gum was restored, and the palate was drawn together. Because of this one surgery, word began spreading throughout the islands that there were Jesus-people who cared, and islanders became increasingly interested in the message of the missionaries.

After about a year of working among lepers in South Korea, Tommy made a brief foray into Taiwan and preached in two different leper colonies. Because several Chinese dialects were spoken, he had to use two interpreters for his messages. This meant that a message took three times as long to preach, but no one was complaining.

Within the next few years, Tommy also traveled to Malaysia and tried to start a work there. However the government clamped down on him immediately. He was told that because Malaysia is officially a Muslim country, Christian ministries were strictly forbidden.

These travels on the part of the Tillmans do not reflect a case of flightiness. One of Tommy's primary goals was to begin a ministry among lepers who had never been reached with the gospel, and he was assessing many different regions.

Finally believers in Malaysia said, "Mr. Tillman, the lepers in Thailand need some help. If you go in there, you will be permitted by the government to work freely among them."

Tommy didn't know how the Malaysians knew of Thailand's need and they gave him few specifics. So he flew into Bangkok and chased around for two weeks asking if anyone—civilians, missionaries, doctors, or government officials—knew anything about leper colonies. No one seemed to have any helpful information.

Tommy was discouraged, but then he located an English language phone book in Bangkok and lugged it back with him to America. From the U.S. he wrote to every hospital serving Bangkok's seventeen million people and asked for information about lepers.

About four weeks later, he received a letter from a Dr. Kanchana and her husband. She wrote, "Brother Tillman, we have been praying for six years that God would send someone to start a work here. We will do the medical work if you do the preaching and building of churches."

Tommy returned to Thailand in 1985 and met the Kanchana family, and the two parties united with the goal of reaching the lepers of Thailand with both spiritual and medical assistance. Though leprosy was very treatable with drugs such as Rifampcin, Dapsone, and Clofazimine, many lepers did not know this and others could not afford care. Thus, many lepers were in horrendous condition.

Initially, Tommy had to spend time identifying with lepers and gaining their acceptance. He began sleeping under bridges with them and in alleys behind store buildings. Gradually they began teaching him the Thai language. He began catching words, phrases, grammar, and how to put sentences together. It was very challenging, but Tommy prayed, "Dear God, you've brought me to these people and I must learn their language. I cannot do this work without a thorough knowledge of it. Please help me!"

Seemingly small encouragements went a long way during this period. A young Buddhist woman named Tip-arpha Mingkhwan was converted. She eventually became one of the greatest evangelizers Tommy had ever known. Everywhere she went she bubbled over with the gospel message. She began a ministry on the campus of Chiang Mai University where over 20,000 students attended. Years later, she would sometimes bring student converts from the university to sing and give testimonies to the young ones at the children's home.

In Tommy's May, 1987, newsletter he wrote, "My life's dream now is to establish a Christian leper colony for the street lepers of Thailand and to build a church right in the middle of the grounds. If you could see the leper mothers with leper children in their arms wandering the streets of Bangkok and Chiangmai...it would break your heart. The Lord has sent us a Christian man and his wife who are willing to manage such a colony. He has been preaching for quite a few years and is very much excited about this opportunity. We also have found a medical doctor who is willing to visit such a leper village two times each week to check the patients."

A year later, the Tillmans and Kanchanas were able to buy five acres of land. They did their own construction work, building a structure that would serve as both hospital and shelter.

Along with the ministry to lepers, Tommy also began noticing the great needs among the Hill Tribe people. He learned that these people often killed their twin babies to please the "spirits". They typically stuffed ashes down their throats until the infants smothered.

Then God opened the doors for the construction of an orphanage and two Hill Tribe churches. Mountain people began attending the churches and brought homeless children. The Tillmans also took in vagabonds off the streets of Bangkok, and leprous parents gave up their children so the young ones wouldn't contract the disease. Though Tommy strenuously objected, the Thais insisted upon naming the orphanage Tillmanville.

Tommy's heart broke as he realized that if he didn't somehow give these children a home many would end up as street children in Bangkok. And Thailand is one of the leading countries in the world for child prostitution.

As the ministry heated up in Thailand, Tommy heard that there might be an opportunity in Vietnam. The Vietnamese government was even interested in speaking with him. So Tommy flew into Vietnam and government officials transported him deep into the Mekong Delta. They suggested the great need of a hospital in that region. However, some underground Christians took him aside and said, "We know this sounds crazy but do not build a hospital here. If you build anything to help the Vietnamese, as soon as it is completed, they will kick you out. Then they will take over the work and thoroughly secularize it."

Tommy is often amazed at how word spreads. A social worker from Vietnam heard about him and located him in Thailand. He told Tommy, "Come back with me into Vietnam. There is much that can still be done for lepers. They are crying out for Bibles."

So Tommy loaded up a big suitcase with Bibles and booked a flight from Bangkok to Ho Chi Minh City. During the flight, he was given a sheet with a list of contraband not allowed into Vietnam. On the list was gospel tracts and Bibles.

There Tommy sat loaded down with Bibles and, of course, he couldn't turn around and go back home. He began to pray and it wasn't a quaint prayer like, "Now I lay me down to sleep..." It was: "Dear God, I'm in a situation here! I have all these Bibles in one hand and in the other a sheet of paper saying I could get into big trouble for this. God, I know I'm not Moses at the Red Sea, and you're going to have to part this sea. Please work some sort of miracle."

They disembarked from the plane in Vietnam and went to customs. There was only one person ahead of Tommy. He prayed, "God, I don't know if I'm headed for jail or what, but help me to be able to face whatever happens with courage."

He stepped up to the customs agents. They glanced him up and down with practiced eyes. "Have you declared that watch and camera?"

"No, am I supposed to?"

"Yes, you must fill out forms on your watch and camera before you can bring them across the border. Go over there and do these forms; then you can enter our country."

Tommy filled out the forms with trembling hands. He glanced over at his bags, but the officials had not opened them yet. When the paperwork was completed, he took it to them.

They said, "Well, go on in, we are through with you."

"Praise the Lord," Tommy said. "Hallelujah!"

The next day a man and his sister showed up on their bicycles to pick up the Bibles. Tommy could see the joy and gratefulness on their faces.

Yet, whenever Tommy wanted to expand the work in Vietnam and build a base of operations or a hospital, the underground believers consistently warned against it. Like the Apostle Paul in Acts, he felt that the Holy Spirit was warning him away from Vietnam at that time.

In late 1988, Tommy was walking down a street in Bangkok when he began experiencing acute chest pain. The pain was so severe he had to sit down on the side of the road.

He prayed, "God, I can hardly draw a breath. I'm really hurting...I can't even stand."

As he prayed, he recalled that Public Bus #15 passes a hospital. Suddenly Bus #15 appeared around the corner. Somehow he waved the bus down and dragged himself onto it. He whispered to the driver: "Pohm my-sa-by mahk! Pah bpy rohng pa-yah-bahn kap" that is, "I am very sick. Take me to a hospital."

When he arrived at the hospital, he could only take baby steps off the bus and through the hospital entrance. He described the pain through clenched teeth and a doctor quickly checked him.

"You're having a heart attack," he said. "We must admit you."

Soon there were needles in his veins and various equipment surrounding his bed. The next morning the doctor came in and displayed his wonderful bedside manner.

"You've had a heart attack and we're not trained for problems of this kind. You will probably die here."

That was great encouragement. Besides this, the hospital personnel proved their dearth of heart expertise when they wheeled in a cart carrying a plate of fried eggs and fried pork chops. Tommy didn't know how a heart victim should be treated so he went ahead and devoured the meal.

Three days later the doctor still seemed clueless about how to handle his problem so Tommy said, "If I'm going to die, doctor, I want to die with my kind of people. I'm going to the leper colony where we have a church."

"Go ahead," said the doctor. "You will probably die."

So three lepers who could still walk came and checked Tommy out of the facility and took him to the leper colony. A Mr. and Mrs. Nu took him into their one-room bamboo home. Mrs. Nu had already lost her limbs, hair, nose, ears, and eyes to leprosy and her husband had contracted it from her. Besides the deformities of leprosy, Mrs. Nu bore awful scars from a stomping her brother had given her when he learned she'd become a Christian.

Tommy prayed, "God, if you are going to take my life at this time, please just let me die here among my people, the lepers."

Meanwhile, Mrs. Nu went out into the forest, searched out healing herbs, and procured nutritious vegetables. With these she made soups and potions. Within weeks Tommy's strength was restored to the extent that he could fly back to America for open heart surgery. United States doctors did a five-way heart bypass and it appeared to be a success.

At about this time, a church approached Tommy. The pastoral search committee said, "You have these serious heart problems now. You should really stay in the U.S. and get the care you need. Would you consider becoming the pastor of our church? We'll take care of the administration, the visitation, church programs, funerals and weddings—all you'll have to do is preach three times a week."

That sounded okay to Tommy so he agreed. The first Sunday he preached and everyone enjoyed it. But as he preached on Wednesday evening, he began feeling uncomfortable. An inner voice seemed to say, *You know you're not a pastor. God called you to be missionary. How can you leave the lepers and orphans God has given you?*

The following Sunday, Tommy resigned. He figured that was the briefest pastorate ever recorded among the Baptists. By the next week, he was back in Thailand.

Chief Sho of the Maya tribe has passed away,
but this is his wife with Tommy. She was converted
and baptized right after her husband.

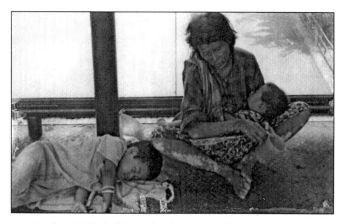

Psalm 142:4: "I looked on my right hand, and behold, but there was no man that would know me; refuge failed me; no man cared for my soul." We will never, as long as I live, forsake the lepers of Thailand. This is a leprous mother with two of her leprous children begging on the streets.

Right after a Sunday morning service at our leper
church at Mae Lao, Thailand. I am at the left, in the
blue shirt, with two of my leper friends.

A Thai man who has lost his legs to leprosy
is baptized.

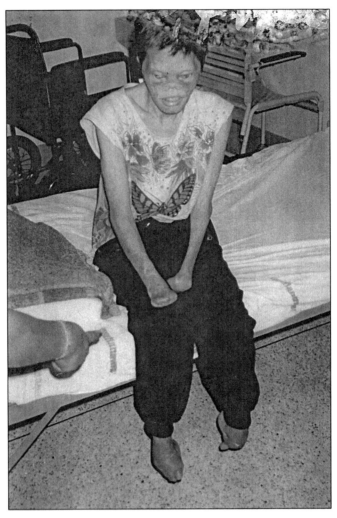

Mrs. Nu, the Thai woman who helped Tommy
recover after a heart attack.

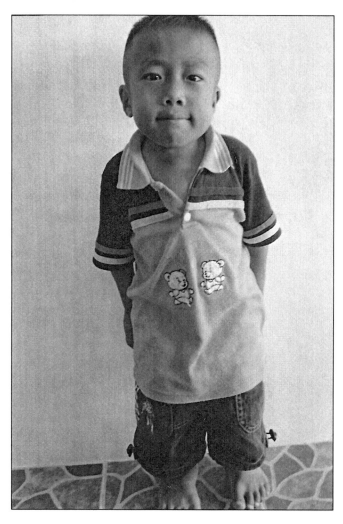

The little boy at the orphanage in Thailand will
never grow any larger. He has a
bone disease.

The orphanage and invalid home - together in
Thailand.

Ion had never had his picture taken until we met
him and his mother.

Some church members in Ulaanbaatar, the capital city of Mongolia. The brother at the far left with the necktie is the pastor and a great soul-winner. Thank the Lord for him.

The woman on the left is a medical doctor at the second mission hospital in Mongolia. The woman to the right is the Mayor's wife who came to Ulaanbaatar seeking someone to teach her how to become a Christian. Now she assists at the hospital.

Tommy with a communist governor in
the Gobi Desert who gave permission to build
the hospital and church. He is giving Tommy
Mongolian clothes to wear.

The third girl from left is the one who prayed for
food and found the feeding station.

Mitch Tillman, with the Mongolian infant he and his wife, Baljmaa, adopted.

Women prisoners coming to a service to hear singing and preaching. They are not forced to come, but voluntarily, even though the place of worship is very cold. Many of these women are there because they killed their husbands.

On the left I Young Suei, the adopted daughter of the Tillmans. The infant in the nurse's arms is Moses, an abandoned infant taken in by the orphanage.

One of the first children's churches in Ulaanbaatar, Mongolia. This is the first day of this new church and they praised the Lord for the good number that attended. The Lord gave Tommy the vision to have a children's church in every neighborhood of this city of 1.25 million people.

Chapter Six

In the early 1990s Tommy began sensing a burden for the people of Mongolia. He was so busy with other projects he tried to ignore the calling, but it only grew in his spirit. Years flew by, yet there seemed to be no possibility of entering the country.

Tommy knew Mongolia was a pro-Communist country, but he still wondered if there was any way to minister there. There was no American embassy in either Thailand or Mongolia at that time, but there happened to be one in Beijing, China. In 1995, he flew to Beijing and tried desperately to obtain a visa into Mongolia. But customs officials said, "You cannot go into this nation unless you have a letter of invitation from some Mongolian company that is recognized by the government. When you obtain this letter of invitation, we will give you a visa."

Tommy returned to Bangkok and months passed. Then one afternoon he was walking the streets of the city and he happened to notice a bookstore. When he entered he almost laughed. The entire bookstore could not have contained more than fifty books. However, he did find a book about Mongolia and he bought it. Inside the book he found the names of many different businesses in Mongolia. So he phoned a Mongolian travel agent.

Tommy said, "Do you speak English?"

"Yes, what can we do for you?"

"Can you get me into Mongolia?"

"Yes, if you will use our business on your round trip to Mongolia, we'll get you in."

Tommy was excited. "Would you send me a letter to that effect?"

When he received the letter, he obtained a visa into Mongolia and set up his flight. When he landed in Ulaan Baatar, the capitol city, the twenty-four year old daughter of the travel agent met him at the airport to act as his interpreter. She introduced herself as Baljmaa. The first thing Tommy said to her after introductions was, "Do you know of any Christians in this country?"

Her eyes grew wide. "Mister, are you a Christian?"

"I sure am."

She said, "I became a Christian two weeks ago and I have been praying that God would help me. Will you teach me everything you know of the Bible doctrines?"

"How did you find out about Jesus?"

She said, "You will not believe it. Fortune tellers are on every street corner in Mongolia because people look to them for hope and guidance. I went to one out of curiosity and she gazed at me for a long time.

Finally she said, 'I can see in your eyes that you are very sad—you are seeking something.'"

Then this woman said the most astounding thing: "You need to open your heart and life up to Jesus, the Christ."

Baljmaa still cannot imagine why a fortune teller would say that but her words placed the girl under conviction to come to Jesus and meet him as her Savior.

Whenever Tommy presents this account, he reiterates his belief that fortune telling is pagan and God has no place for it. He himself tested a fortune teller by asking if she could tell him his name and, of course, she could not. However, God will never be limited and if he can use a donkey to speak his word, he can use anyone.

Tommy has found multiplied times that it is the Word of God that makes a Christian effective. He states, "The Word of God convicts and convinces of the truth in soul winning. If you wish to be a spiritual Sunday school teacher, teach the Word of God. If you wish to be an effective pastor, simply preach the Word of God."

Tommy marveled that God would bring Baljmaa and him together at just the right time. During his first month in Mongolia, Tommy spent much time teaching the girl. She finally took him to meet her father who was a Communist. Amazingly, the father displayed a growing interest in the Bible and in Christianity. Eventually he actually became a Christian and now serves as a pastor under Tommy's leadership in Mongolia.

This may seem amazing that a Communist leader would make such an about face, but Tommy has seen the Word of God stand on its own effectively many times. He tells of a man named Ted Rollan who was imprisoned for selling drugs. He ended up in the same jail cell as an atheist who happened to know some memorized Scripture. The man enjoyed quoting the Bible, jeering, and poking fun at it. One day Ted sat on the floor of the cell watching as the atheist paced the floor, spouting Scripture disdainfully. The Holy Spirit used those Scriptures to convict Ted's heart. He stood up abruptly and said, "You know what? I'm a sinner and I want to be saved." He prayed and invited Christ into his heart and was born again in a jail cell with a Bible-scorning atheist. It is in the Word of God that the power resides; not in our dynamism, eloquence, or salesmanship.

This is why the Word of God and the knowledge of it is at the very center of everything Harbor Evangelistic International does. Once, a man boasted to Tommy that he reads the Bible through twice every year. As Tommy thought about it, he acknowledged that it's important to read the entire Bible, not just parts of it. But he purposed that he'd continue his practice of reading the Bible through once about every four years. He now tells the churches he visits, "Remember, reading and studying the Bible is not a race—it's not just threading words through your eyes. It is reading each word, each detail, understanding it, and doing what it says."

In a December, 1993, prayer letter, Tommy wrote of another appeal from Vietnam: "I just received a letter from an underground Christian in Vietnam and the lepers are wanting me back there again as soon as possible. These are the ones the Communist government has placed in the jungles to die." But Tommy was unable to enter the country at that time; his ministry there was confined to prayer.

In 1995, Larry Gue of Decatur Baptist Church in Alabama led a short-term missions team to visit and assist Tommy's ministry in Thailand. Gue had already accompanied him on three other mission trips.

Of this visit, Gue wrote, "I was overwhelmed. I never grasped in reality all that God has done in Thailand. As you may know, Tommy's ministry with the lepers is an unbelievable one. The leper churches are flourishing and the leper colony far exceeded anything that could be imagined."

But then Gue began describing "Tillmanville", the 11-acre ministry to orphans. "The ministry that Brother Tommy and his co-ministers Rick and Srichand Horn have begun is beyond belief. These orphans, many of which are the children of lepers, are given a safe, clean place to live. The staff are able to adopt these children, teach them about Jesus and His love for them, and train them to be future pastors, teachers, or godly businessmen who will spread the Good News of Jesus Christ wherever they go."

Gue went on to mention many pressing needs Tommy faced at that time: a children's dormitory, a diesel generator, a church building, housing for the

Tillmans, and money to feed and clothe the growing number of orphans.

Another young lady came to Thailand on a short-term mission opportunity from a church in Franklin, Tennessee. She told Tommy, "How can I suffer for Jesus while I'm here? I want to be able to go back to my home church and tell them I didn't just try to take it easy."

Tommy said, "I don't know how to answer that. Just try to serve in any way you're needed."

A few weeks later, she came to him and said, "I think I'm learning a little about suffering for Christ."

He looked at her and saw that she had one of the worst cases of head lice he'd ever seen.

She'd been working with the children being admitted into the orphanage. Most of them come from the most unsanitary conditions. They live in utter squalor, even sleeping inside huts with pigs and goats (who are kept there for fear the animals will be stolen). They contract all sorts of disease, including head lice.

Tommy joked, "Young lady, if you're not careful you won't just suffer. Those lice will martyr you before you can get back home."

The lepers' and orphans' dietary tastes were not exactly of the gourmet type. For example, in June, 1995, Tommy mentioned their menu for three days. "One day," he reported, "we had dog meat with the lepers, the next day we had fried ant eggs with the orphans, and the third day of the week we fried the ants themselves. People also love cicadas, silkworms, bamboo worms, and, most of all, grasshop-pers. Some of the workers caught a nine-foot snake but never offered to cook it for us (thank God). They took it home for their own meal."

Tommy finally got the opportunity to go back and visit Mrs. Nu and her husband. She is the leper who nursed him back to health after the heart attack.

As Tommy crossed the rice paddies a few hundred yards from the Nu's home, he called, "Brother and Sister Nu. It's been so long. I'm back to see you."

He heard excited voices. "Husband, husband, it is Tommy. I go to meet him."

"Wait. Me too."

Tommy could see Mrs. Nu in the distance vaulting out of her house and down the steps. Halfway down, she misplaced her elbow and down she went onto her face. But then she was up again, calling, "Tommy, I love you. You told me about Jesus."

Now she was actually running on her elbows and knees trying to follow his voice. Her husband was not far behind.

When she reached Tommy, she raised her sight-less face upward. He saw the deep, empty eye sockets, the rotted teeth, the missing facial features. Then he glimpsed the scars on her forehead and on the arm and leg stumps—scars her Buddhist brother had given her when she was converted.

Tommy picked her up in his arms and she gave him a kiss. He saw tears slipping from the hollow eye sockets. He held her away from his body and exam-ined her again. Now here was a woman who bore the marks of Jesus on her body.

In August of the same year, Tommy wrote home of his sadness regarding a loss: "Little Mon Nee, a sweet eight-year-old girl, died at the orphanage a few weeks ago. We could not bury her at the orphanage; she had to be buried under a termite hill. This was the only area the Buddhist government would allow space for her burial."

On a brighter note, he added, "Mon Nee was saved and baptized only a week before her death. Her brother, who lives at the orphanage, has been called to preach the gospel so we praise the Lord for this."

In December, Tommy wrote that money had been provided to purchase five additional acres for the orphanage, and to complete a second dormitory for the children and furnish it.

In early 1996 the ministry was booming with a large leper colony in Mae Lao, colonies in Prapadange, the orphanage at Nong Loom, and eleven leper churches spread throughout Thailand. Tommy also made contact with the Karen Long-Neck Tribes in the high mountains of northern Thailand. Tommy and his staff began studying their religion so that they could approach and witness to these tribes more effectively.

While Jo Ann recovered from knee surgery she sent out a prayer letter in which she reported that Tommy and his team were finally able to travel to Vietnam again in response to pleas from the underground church.

That summer, Richard Guay and Barbara Soucy from Knoxville, Tennessee, and Mr. and Mrs. Dennis

Crutchfield flew to Thailand and assisted for several months with the ministry. Assistance such as this enabled the staff to reach out to unreached areas. They founded a church in an Akah village located far back in the mountains. By August, fifteen churches had been established, including a new one with an attendance of eighteen just outside of Bangkok.

Tommy realized anew how important it is to continue praying for people and "not to faint." He had been praying for and witnessing to a Buddhist taxi driver in Chiang Mai for years. He'd half joke with the man about Buddha's father being an elephant while Christ's father was the Spirit of God. Apparently there's a quote in Buddhist writings that reads, "...for twenty years they had no children. But one night Queen Maya (Buddha's mother) had a strange dream in which she saw a white elephant entering into her womb through the right side of the chest and she became pregnant. The king and the people looked forward with anticipation for the birth of the royal child" (Buddha).

One day Tommy took the taxi driver out to visit the children's home. The man was so astonished that the next day he brought his wife to the orphanage, and they stayed for the singing and preaching service. They said they'd never in their lives seen children as happy as these orphans. Tommy believed the couple was very close to being converted; he also believed that reaching the Thai children was the best way to reach the nation for Christ.

Near the close of 1996 Tommy wrote that inflation was hitting hard in Thailand and the cost of food was tripling. There were now about eighty orphans in the children's home, and it cost about $100 per day to feed the lepers and orphans.

One morning the staff leader of the orphanage came to Tommy and said, "Mr. Tillman, there is no money and no food for the children today."

Tommy said, "Are you sure there's nothing up in a cupboard somewhere?"

"There is nothing," she said. "Should we go ask anyone for money?"

"No, let's wait and let God work."

A little while later, the Buddhist foreman of the construction work on the mission compound walked up to him.

He said, "We have seen all the children you take care of. The workers decided to put some money together, and we will feed your children today."

Time after time, God provided, often in unexpected ways.

Tommy says, "Some of my Baptist brothers who sleep with three-piece suits on, raise their starched eyebrows and say, 'You would take money from Buddhists for God's work?'

"You bet I would," says Tommy. "Haven't you read the Scripture in Luke where Jesus says, 'Make yourselves friends by use of the mammon of unrighteousness so that when it fails, converts shall receive you into eternal habitations'?"

Tommy was very encouraged by a huge provision in another area. The cost for wiring and setting up the children's home with electricity was placed at $40,000. Near the beginning of November the electric company began digging holes for the power poles. Within weeks, Tommy learned that the cost for the entire project was being underwritten. They would owe nothing!

As 1997 dawned, stories abounded of individuals rescued and helped. A nineteen-year-old girl named Young Suei was brought in. She was paralyzed and had been bedridden for ten years. Her father left her at the hospital and never returned even to check on her. The hospital where she lay paid her twenty cents a day to do sewing for them, but her treatment was very poor.

A mother of three young girls from a hill tribe was converted and refused to remain in a home where her husband continually worshipped and gave offerings to pagan spirits. When she moved out of the house her husband flew into a rage and killed her and then himself. The girls were lovingly admitted to the orphanage.

Staff members found a child named Ion and his mother living by the side of a dirt road not far from the orphanage. The father had given his wife AIDS and then abandoned her. When she gave birth to Ion, he also contracted AIDS passed on by his mother. On May 30, 1997 Ion's mother passed away and on December 27 Ion also died of AIDs complications. The good news is that both believed in Jesus and had trusted him for salvation.

Then a desperate prayer request: Two sisters named Nam Wan and Nam Phong, who legally belonged in the orphanage, had been kidnapped by their father. The police reported locating him, but then he disappeared again. It was believed he planned to sell them in exchange for drugs.

About a month later, Nam Wan was located. She was skinny, filthy, and had burns all over her. When a child of the Hill people gets sick she is burned with the tip of a red-hot stick, supposedly to chase out the evil spirits. Nothing was ever heard of Nam Phong and the staff trembled for her prospects.

Tommy was horrified when he saw the poverty in parts of Mongolia. For example, he went to the city dump on the edge of Ulaan Baatar. Eighty thousand people a day sent their garbage to that foul place. Tommy watched as trucks dumped the bodies of dead, rotting cattle, dogs, and other animals. He saw people shoving and fighting to be the first to cut putrid meat off the carcasses. Meat like this was a luxury to them.

With sadness and tragedy all around, touches of humor now and then provided a few moments of comic relief. Through the years, Tommy had put on a few pounds and had a bit of a paunch. One day he was walking the city streets in Mongolia. He noticed a woman behind him but thought nothing of it. After crossing several streets and walking a few alleys, he saw she was still there, and he became a little concerned. He stopped and sat on a bench, and she sat down not far away. He went and grabbed a bite at a food stand, and she stood and watched. Finally, he walked up to her and said, "Lady, are you following me?"

"Yes," she said.

"But why? I'm a married man."

"Oh, I'm married too," she said. "That's no problem."

"But I'm a Christian missionary. It doesn't look good for me to be followed around by women."

"But I like you," she said.

"Why do you like me? I'm not available."

"Because, mister," she said, "you look just like Buddha."

Tommy thought, *I know Jesus said to be all things to all men, but this is ridiculous! Thank God, someday I'll have a new body and I won't look like Buddha anymore.*

The year 1998 turned out to be an amazing year of God's wonders. Tommy wanted to build a hospital in Mongolia but the Communist government would not allow it. So Tommy and a fellow Christian traveled down through the Gobi desert to talk to the Communist leadership of the region face to face. There were no roads and it took eighteen grueling hours to travel two hundred miles.

They met the governor of the area and he stubbornly resisted their request. However, Tommy and his friend were able to spend some time with the governor's family. He learned that one of his daughters was a dentist in Ulaan Baatar. Tommy recalled that Jesus said for his followers to be wise as serpents, yet harmless as doves. So when he returned to the city, he decided to try using a little of that wisdom. He met the woman, befriended her, and began describing his work in Mongolia. In time, she started displaying interest in the Christian message, and eventually she was converted and baptized. She then was instrumental in convincing her father to allow the hospital.

Before long, an eighteen-room hospital was completed and her father went to China and bought the X-ray equipment and other furnishings and equipment for a hospital. Tommy called the dentist daughter of the Communist governor and asked her to be the hospital administrator. This development impressed the governor tremendously. He sent his personal limousine and chauffeur to pick Tommy up and transport him to his estate.

He said, "Mr. Tillman, because you are honoring my daughter and taking good care of her, you go ahead and preach your gospel all you want and I offer my protection."

In time, two other medical doctors were converted and three Christian nurses joined them to assist. They also hired a full-time stoker to keep the furnace fire going twenty-four hours a day because winter temperatures in the Gobi Desert average thirty to forty degrees below zero. Every patient who entered the hospital received a Bible in their language and a presentation of the gospel.

Tommy knew that only God could do some-thing like this and he went away filled with joy. Missionaries would sometimes say to him, "We feel led to build a church or hospital. What can we do? We have no finances."

His answer was, "First, make sure your hearts are right with God and there is no corner of besetting sin. Then begin preaching and teaching the people when- ever and wherever you can. Third, get a shovel, a pick, and a hoe and go out and dig the foundation for the building. Then pray, "God, we've gone as far as we can go. We must have your help now!" Over and over Tommy saw God provide in situations like this.

Young Suei, the paralytic victim whom Tommy had met and transported to their hospital became a Christian believer. Twelve years had passed since her family had abandoned her and no one ever came to visit her. Government funds that had paid for her care in McLean Rehabilitation Center had run out and authorities planned to transfer her to a rest home outside of Bangkok allegedly controlled by Thai Mafia. Tommy was told she would not survive there for long. He and Jo Ann decided to adopt Young into their family and thus take responsibility for her care and all costs associated with it. The adoption was finalized in November and Young Suei was radiant. Tommy hired a young girl whose job it was to care for Young twenty-four hours a day.

Also in late 1998, Tommy trekked far into the Mongolian mountains and found what, to him, was an unusual diet. The people ate occasional sheep and goat meat and drank horse milk, but ate no vegeta- bles and drank no water. After drinking horse milk for two days, he experienced an acute allergic reac- tion and had to return to Ulaan Bataar where he was hospitalized.

In his travels, however, Tommy began noticing the need for an orphanage. The government did administrate scattered orphanages, but he struggled with their policies. They'd gather about 150 children and devote one hour per day to teaching them a trade such as carpentry, masonry, sewing or cooking. They fed them one paltry meal and then turned them loose on the streets to find a place to sleep. One night Tommy trailed some children and saw them pull up manhole covers and crawl down into the city sewers to sleep.

Tommy petitioned the government in September, 1998, to allow him to establish an orphanage, and officials were pleased. They allowed him to travel the country as a diplomat, and they actually offered him a sizeable piece of land free of charge. He was thrilled until parliament members began sharing the conditions. First, they mandated a ten-mile paved road to the property. They drew up blueprints for a complex that would cost $800,000 to build. Environmental headquarters declared that they could shut the orphanage down at any time if they disagreed with the standards. But, worst of all, they stated that the school must hire mostly Communist teachers with only a few Christians permitted.

Tommy politely refused the land and purposed that he'd allow God to give them a children's home in His own way. He sensed what he believed was a Satanic spirit of depression at this point. A voice in his mind seemed to say: *You fool. You already owe huge expenditures to support the churches, leper colonies,*

*and children's home in Thailand. How can you even
dream of launching a ministry in Mongolia?*

But then, in early December he opened a letter
from Jack Chick of Chick Tracts and found a $20,000
check for the work in Mongolia. Tommy and Jo Ann
knew unquestionably at this point that God wanted
them to expand into that region.

The Tillman's hurt for the children when now, for
the first time, Buddhists began throwing rocks and
dirt at them, calling them vulgar names and challenging them to fight. In a land that is 98% Buddhist,
Tommy knew it would do little good to complain to
Buddhist leaders.

By February, 1999, God had already raised up
seven Mongolian believers to develop the work in
this nation. Their names were Tsogt-Erdene Khorloo,
Otgoo, Uurtsaikh, Ouynchimeg, Mendsaikhan,
Ouynjargal, and, of course, Baljmaa. Though difficult names even for Tommy to pronounce, he knew
they were now carefully recorded with the correct
spelling in the Lamb's Book of Life.

The following month, there was a heartbreak in
one of the Thai children's homes. A young 14-year-
old named Thumb died of cancer complications. He
had surrendered his life to preach the gospel, but God
obviously wanted the brave boy to serve in His very
presence.

Tommy was amazed at times upon hearing of
the germination and growth of mere seeds planted
in various locations. Many years earlier, he had been
instrumental in the founding of a children's home in the
Philippines. When he moved on to Thailand, he turned

the fledgling work over to a veteran missionary already in the Philippines. The work grew and in the spring of 1999 Tommy received a letter from a believer on the Island of Samar, Philippines. This convert had learned of Tommy and wanted to go out under the auspices of Harbor International and evangelize among the lepers scattered throughout the jungles. Tommy agreed to begin supporting him financially.

That summer Tommy made a trip back to the U.S. and when he returned to Mongolia he carried four boxes of gospel tracts in his luggage. This time, customs officials detected them and caused a great uproar as they condemned him for seeking to smuggle propaganda into the country. Fortunately, though they confiscated the tracts, they still allowed Tommy to cross the border.

But then, some good news. A prominent Mongolian business-man committed his life to Christ. His name was Mr. Luvsan-Ochir Dondog, and armed with CPA and Ph.D. degrees, he was president of the Mongolian Institute for Certified Public Accountants. He expressed great interest in visiting the mission churches and assisting with the ministry to the children.

Uurtsaikh, one of the native Mongolian missionaries, began evangelizing door-to-door in Gobi Desert villages. She reported a remarkable openness to the gospel. However, she often approached homes with trepidation because almost every home had a guard dog and these dogs could be savage. One man was bitten badly when he tried to protect Uurtsaikh from attack.

Chapter Seven

It would be impossible to name all the individuals who now served in some capacity in the burgeoning ministries in South Korea and the Philippines or, much more prominently, in Thailand and Mongolia. Besides others mentioned, Mr. Suwat, with his wife, served as pastor for the Prapadange Leper Colony, Pope Srichai evangelized throughout the region, and in July, the Alford family of Swannsboro, North Carolina arrived to assist. Srichai was one of the highest ranking Buddhists in Thailand before his conversion and became one of the best evangelists Tommy knew at witnessing to Buddhists.

By August, 1999, property had been purchased high in the mountains of Thailand and a church was constructed for the Ahka Hill people.

A month later, Tommy took a party into the Gobi desert on an evangelism mission. One night a whipping wind snatched away three of the tents. The group searched in a frigid rain for any covered spot that might contain camel dung dry enough to burn for heat. They suffered through the night and then drove hard for eighteen hours to reach their destination. Tommy went to preach in one town while an associate, Larry Gue, preached in a village about a quarter of a mile away. Communist officials appeared at Tommy's meeting and shut him down, but this apparently distracted them enough that Gue preached unimpeded for several hours.

The government began telling village residents to run from Christian missionaries, claiming they teach converts to commit suicide. Perhaps officials were misinterpreting Christian scriptures such as those that speak of dying to selfish ambition or being crucified with Christ.

Communists also cracked down on child evangelism, demanding that street children not be exposed to the gospel. However, they did refer acute cases of malnutrition or neglect to Tommy, asking only that he find homes for them. Tommy's staff then gladly placed them in Christian homes.

In October, 1999, Tommy reported the purchase of ten more rai for the children's home. One acre equals about 2.5 rai. This set the total acres for the Thai orphanage at sixty. He now believed they owned enough land to begin a farm at which the boys could be taught efficient farming principles. A school was also now established in the children's home so that the children would not be required to attend Buddhist or pagan public schools.

By this point, twenty-one churches had been founded in Thailand, though some were no longer directly under the auspices of Harbor International because Tommy tried to push churches toward being indigenous as quickly as was feasible.

In early 2000, Tommy praised God that the Mongolian taxi driver to whom he had witnessed for over ten years finally forsook Buddha for Jesus. Tommy wondered what would have happened if he'd given up on the man years earlier.

Enclosed with a prayer letter, Tommy sent a graphic photo of a six-year-old Mongolian girl. From her feet to her young face, she was covered with scars, bruises and bite marks inflicted by her father. Fortunately she was rescued by the children's home staff before her father killed her. Tommy's challenge to western Christians was that when they see polished travel documentaries of the beautiful country of Mongolia, they must not forget the atrocities that regularly occur behind the scenes.

That spring, Tommy reported a Mongolian winter that was one of the most severe on record. It was estimated that 1.6 million head of livestock froze to death, and a mass famine was eminent. Little other livelihood existed for the average Mongolian besides cattle.

A young Communist girl had grown up in a home in which God was denied and Jesus was blasphemed. One day, she was wandering the desert with no food or money. Finally she prayed, "If there is a God, please help me now. I have no food and I'm starving to death."

The next day she came upon one of the mission's food stations. They gave her so much food, her shrunken stomach couldn't even eat it all.

She became a Christian, claiming, "These Christians loved me so much, I knew they spoke the truth. I had to be saved."

Tommy told of a woman named Ouynjargal who worked with the mission in the Gobi Desert. The woman was dying of an incurable lung disease and the doctors gave her only months to live. Besides this, she was receiving regular nomad threats of rape and bodily harm. Yet she refused to stop serving the Lord, and she led fifty individuals to salvation in March. Shigshee, another Mongolian street evangelist, covered up to five miles a day, spreading the gospel among the nomad population.

In May, Tommy spent some time with his adopted daughter, Young Suei, checked on progress in the Prapadange Leper Colony, and devoted some time to Mr. and Mrs. Nu, special friends among the lepers. At a Sunday service for lepers, a male leper limped pitifully to the pulpit. He said, "Look at me—my body is rotting away and I'm losing my sight, but today I must tell you that I am glad that I'm a leper." Gasps were heard in the crowd.

He said, "I used to be the most profane blasphemer with a vulgar tongue and a dirty story for every occasion. I made fun of Christians unmercifully. Then I got sick and had to go to the doctor.

He said, 'Sir, you are a leper. If a disease like tuberculosis doesn't kill you first, the leprosy will eventually destroy your whole body.'"

The man paused. "That is the day I fell on my knees and begged God for mercy and I cried out for Jesus Christ to save me. I would rather be here with leprosy than to be a healthy blasphemer and sinner."

After this inspiring respite, as sometimes happens, Satan had to offset the blessings with some unexplainable opposition. Tommy and a few others planned to fly into Mongolia to make plans regarding the children's home. However, when they arrived in South Korea, they found the flight into Mongolia to be postponed. Korean officials claimed that China was flying incorrect patterns, thus violating their air space. After staying in a hotel for four days, they again went to the airport for an announced flight to Mongolia, and this time it was cancelled for at least a week. The party was forced to fly back into Thailand and from there through Beijing, China, into Mongolia.

Several months later, the hospital officials at McKean Rehabilitation Center in Chiang Mai requested that Tommy become the chaplain there. This hospital had a capacity of 400 patients with at least half at any given time devout Buddhists. Amazingly, the hospital directors were saying that Tommy had the authority to witness to anyone at anytime about Jesus. Floored by this development, Tommy purposed that if there was any way his schedule would allow it, he'd take the chaplaincy.

Near the beginning of September the Harbor staff submitted an ad in the Thai newspaper urging anyone who was interested in learning about God and his

Son, Jesus Christ, to write or call. Over one hundred letters and telephone calls came in and this became a monthly project.

Added to this, $100 per month was made available for a Christian radio broadcast, and Pope Srichai began preaching the gospel on Thai radio. Within weeks five hundred phone calls and letters of inquiry came in. In one week alone, the staff learned for sure of eleven individuals who had accepted the Lord Jesus as Savior.

At this time, fifteen young Thai men were studying toward the pastorate or a career in evangelism. Upon graduation, these would be sent into the mountains to the many Hill tribes who were quite open to the gospel.

On November 29, 2000, word came that Mrs. Nu, the woman who helped nurse Tommy back to health after his first heart attack, was now dying. She urgently pleaded to see him. It took Tommy two days to travel from Bangkok to Chiang Rai where Mrs. Nu lived. Pope Srichai intercepted him before he reached the home.

"Sister Nu has just gone on to the Heaven," he said. "She is gone."

Mr. Nu also came out to meet him. He had cared for his wife like a baby for many years. He wept when he saw what a beautiful funeral celebration was planned for her.

At the memorial service Tommy said, "I expect to spend the first few million years in Heaven fellowshipping with Mrs. Nu and she will be able to see me for the first time in her life."

In January, 2001, Tommy's prayer letter listed all the ministries being carried on through Harbor International.

- Bible school with nineteen students studying toward full-time Christian service.
- A radio ministry broadcasting the gospel across Thailand.
- A church building in northern Thailand that will seat over 300 people.
- A leper colony for Christian lepers who have no home nor relatives.
- A children's home housing about 100 children.
- A second children's home being built in northern Thailand about 200 miles from the first one. The dormitories for the new home will house 300 children.
- Twenty-seven churches founded in twenty-two years. Some are now self-supporting.
- A second church is being built in Ulaan Baatar, the capitol of Mongolia.
- A church is being built in western Mongolia in a town with 150,000 people and no other church.
- Four full-time missionaries evangelize in the Gobi Desert in Mongolia.
- A small children's work in Mongolia.

Tommy reminded supporters, however, that effective mission work consists of far more than evangelism and church planting. Now it was winter again in Mongolia, average temperatures were –40 F, and food for dwindling numbers of cattle was scarce. Harbor Evangelism International donated $750 toward food for the cattle.

In March, Tommy complimented his grandson, Zachary Peluso, for short-term service with Harbor International. Zack had visited Thailand twice and his interest had grown with each passing year.

The following month, Tommy wrote supporters that twenty-five new converts were baptized in Mongolia and, in Thailand, the Ulaan Baatar church now averaged ninety people per service.

Two students graduated from the Thai Bible school and were ready to pastor churches. The first, Pastor Nitipat would be going south to Suratthanee Province, where twenty-six individuals had been converted and desperately needed some leadership and nurture. Pastor Veragoon would pastor a Lisa Hill tribe village high in the mountain country.

During the summer twenty children were admitted to the Tillmanville orphanage and every one of them had now received Jesus as Savior.

Near the beginning of August, Tommy began feeling twinges of pain in his chest and he recognized them as possible precursors of another heart attack. To be safe, he returned to the United States for an examination.

Chapter Eleven

On the night of August 29, 2001, Tommy was awakened by major chest pain. It was so severe his medication wouldn't even touch it. Jo Ann rushed him to Hancock Medical Center where he was transferred to Memorial Hospital in Gulfport, Missouri. Immediately they took him into surgery and doctors found several clogged arteries. However, doctors were only able to place a stent in one artery. By September 1, they were able to remove the nitroglycerin drip and start him on oral medication.

Then on Tuesday, October 9, Tommy was again admitted into a hospital, this time in Slidell, Louisiana, and two stents were placed in the main artery to his heart which was almost completely blocked. On November 8, he returned to the hospital, where they placed two additional stents in other arteries. All this was, of course, quite traumatic but he reported feeling better than he had in at least five years.

Following this surgery, Tommy wrote supporters that his desire and goal was to return to service by

December. Tommy's work had piqued the interest of his heart specialist and the man said he'd like to visit Thailand and Mongolia. Tommy joked that just as the apostle Paul had Luke the physician, he would have his own personal heart doctor traveling the world with him.

Meanwhile, back in Thailand 1,000 letters arrived at the radio station in November expressing interest in being born again. Also, one of the Bible students crossed the river into Laos and preached to crowds and was astounded when 150 people were saved.

On a more somber note, Tommy said that he'd undergone his fourth surgery in eight weeks so doctors could add a few more stents to clogged arteries. Still, doctors optimistically claimed that he might make it back to Thailand by December and he did.

Upon his return to Thailand, Tommy baptized twenty-seven new converts and two days later his assistant baptized seventeen more.

Born again doctors were actually approaching Tommy with the desire to serve in a Christian hospital if one could be built in Mongolia's Gobi Desert. He saw the potential a hospital could have in this region, not only to heal people physically but to redeem them spiritually.

Then in late December one of Tommy's heart stents collapsed and he had to return to the U.S. and remain there for almost two months. However the good news is that doctors started him on a new medication reputed to help dissolve plaque in the arteries.

The young girl who Tommy had hired for Young Suei's care had been doing a wonderful job.

However, now Tommy received word that as she traveled between Burma and Thailand, she'd stepped on a land mine. Shrapnel passed through her leg but her life was spared and she was recovering well.

In February and March of 2002, four additional Mongolian believers volunteered to serve in the Gobi Desert, four new rooms were added to the Prapadange Leper Colony in Thailand, and fifty more people turned to Christ as Savior.

Construction on the children's dormitory that would house up to 300 orphans was now almost completed, and 200 children were projected to attend a Thai camp meeting for two weeks in April.

Baljmaa wrote a letter to Tommy describing the activities of her and her father on a Saturday and Sunday. On Saturday morning at 10:00 they had a Chinese language class, at 11:00, taught a Bible study on the Resurrection, at noon, began an English study group in which they read about the Crucifixion of Christ. Then at 1:00 Baljmaa sang with the children and taught them two Bible stories about Jacob.

On Sunday at 10:00 a.m. there was a Chinese language class, at 11:00 a Bible class was taught, at noon Baljmaa's father preached a sermon entitled "No Remission without Blood." And at 1:00 the church celebrated Easter day with a dinner of Chinese food. This was a typical weekend schedule.

Baljmaa's Mongolian language skills were excellent but she was still working on her English. Describing the reasonable price of the Chinese food, she wrote, "For one food, $3, and one food ate two people."

In April, Tommy was still making appeals for a nomad hospital in the Gobi Desert. He knew the hospital would be built in Erdenedalai Sum, about 200 miles from Ulaan Baatar. He also had the blue-prints drawn up, but no money.

Then within two brief weeks the $22,000 for the hospital was donated and a doctor was ready to step in immediately as hospital administrator. By October, the construction was complete. The hospital contained eighteen rooms and was staffed by three full-time doctors and two nurses. The first twelve patients had already been treated.

On a personal note, Tommy made reference to his oldest son: "Mitchell thought he was saved years ago, but recently was truly born again into God's family. The Lord is speaking to his heart about working in this ministry. Please pray for the Lord's leading in his life."

A month later Mitch wrote to U.S. churches, "For forty-seven years I lived as an unbeliever, walking through this world without Christ as my Savior. I have now visited Thailand and Mongolia with my father and I know in my heart that the Lord convicted me of my sins and saved my soul for this purpose. I am planning to take Mongolian language lessons and I'm looking for Bibles in the Mongolian language…"

Meanwhile Tommy was spending some time at the Prapadange Leper Colony. A paralysis victim named Earth rolled up to him in her wheel chair and handed him an envelope. She said, "I want to help the Lord's work at the hospital in the Gobi Desert."

Tommy's heart was crushed when he opened the envelope and found 300 Thai baht equalling about $7.42 U.S., an enormous amount for an impoverished Thai.

He wrote, "We never beg for money. If the Lord wants something done, we know He will furnish the finances. If the money doesn't come, then we believe it is not of God at the time."

In January, 2003, there was a 412-child list of young ones from the hill tribes waiting to enter the children's home in Chiang Rei, and Tommy wished they had the room and the money to take them all in. But space was limited and it cost $70 per month to feed, lodge, and clothe one child.

The reach of the radio station based in Thailand was expanding and now they were also broadcasting the gospel into Burma, Cambodia, and Laos. One hundred and fifty individuals indicated during this month that they were accepting Christ into their lives. Then in February, 170 individuals wrote to radio headquarters claiming to place their faith in Christ alone. Follow up was done through home Bible study courses.

In view of new convert tallies such as these, Tommy wished to assure supporters that there was no trickery, number tampering, or naivete involved. He wrote, "I absolutely cannot, under conviction of the Holy Spirit, count converts if they know little to nothing of sin, the deity of Christ, the virgin birth, and Christ's death and resurrection. We must be very careful because many nationals will do anything an American asks them to do. Some would raise a hand or send in a response if asked to invite Mickey Mouse into their hearts. I could easily report 500 or more conversions each month, but we offer Bibles and growth aids and watch and wait to see if professing Christians begin growing and maturing as believers."

Thus, Tommy can never be accused as a proponent of what some call "easy-believism". He preaches the gospel message in totality: repentance from sin, faith in Christ and His work alone, and, thereby, the permanent indwelling presence of the Holy Spirit, with baptism as a memorial and an act of obedience.

At one point, a church threatened to drop Tommy's support because he preached repentance. He approached the pastor and asked him about it point blank, attempting to show him all the scriptures regarding repentance.

The pastor replied, "But, friend, we're now living in a different dispensation."

Tommy said, "Then maybe John three-sixteen isn't meant for us either. Maybe that's for a different dispensation."

The pastor's jaw hardened and his eyes turned to flint.

"I'm asking you to drop my support," said Tommy. "I can't be affiliated with a church that doesn't preach the whole counsel of God."

The next week five other churches volunteered to begin supporting his ministry.

Near the end of January, Tommy headed back to the U.S. for two more arterial stents, making a total of seven. Then about ten days after this, doctors planned to place a stent in a neck artery. However, on February 10 he experienced another mini-heart attack and doctors added three stents instead of two.

In Mongolia, Mitch was experiencing his first bitter taste of a Mongolian winter. He told Tommy that anyone who believes in global warming should come and spend a month or two in Mongolia.

One afternoon he was out doing errands and he happened to meet a man who knew English. Mitch was doubly surprised. First, few roamed the streets in winter because of the below zero temperatures. Second, almost none knew English. While waiting for a light to change, the pair began a conversation. The talk moved to the topic of Jesus and Mitch briefly explained the gospel. Rarely had Mitch ever seen a heart so open and searching as this man's. The man prayed to receive Christ right there on the street. Mitch invited him to Sunday services in the Mongolian church, half wondering if the profession of faith would prove genuine. But come Sunday morning, there the man was in the service. He stood up before the congregation beaming, and told them he had been born again. Mitch gave him a new Bible and allowed him to officially join the church when baptized.

Given that there are only three months per year in Mongolia in which the weather is even somewhat temperate, that is when any baptisms must take place. Mitch had sixteen converts to baptize in July. The baptismal service was held at a river that flows out of the mountains.

Mitch wrote, "Believe me when I tell you that this was the coldest water I have ever touched. After barely twenty minutes in that water, I was completely numb from the chest down. But we praise God for the sixteen new Christians, all of whom are very active in the church." He and Tommy figured a conversion had to be genuine for a convert to agree to immersion in such frigid waters.

Mitch was learning things about Gobi nomad beliefs from his dad. Many nomads worship nature and when one of their number dies, he or she is left in the desert for the birds and other animals to devour. In that way, the dead return to the god of nature. Mitch knew it would be difficult to convince some that nature is not to be worshipped but the Creator of all nature.

Another thing about Mongolia to which Mitch had to become accustomed was the fact that it was frigid for ten months of the year, sometimes dipping to 40 or 50 below zero. There are over 100,000 coal stoves in the capitol city alone. Besides this, there is a coal power plant in the middle of the city, and at night or early in the morning the coal smoke is so thick it's difficult to see more than a few feet ahead.

Twenty desperate Thai orphans were offered to Tommy for care. Their fate was not certain if they did not receive housing. At first he declined. Harbor Evangelism was already struggling to care for 115 children. But then, during Tommy's prayer time, the Holy Spirit began speaking to him, *"Who is your God? Does He not own it all?"* Then a Scripture rushed into his mind, "Suffer the little children to come unto me, and forbid them not; for of such is the kingdom of God."

Tommy told the home administrator to receive the children into the home. The very next day he received a check in the mail for $11,600.

During the summer of 2003 Tommy's daughter, Teresa, took the opportunity to publicize to all the churches an internet club started by a Reverend Jim Barlow who had served for a time with Tommy. The 742 Club was a children's club founded in honor of a Thai paralysis victim named Earth who had donated an amount equaling $7.42 to the Mongolian ministry. The appeal was for individuals who would be willing to send $7.42 per month to the children of Thailand.

"The amount can even be dedicated in the name of your child or grandchild," Teresa wrote, "and a certificate will be mailed in their name. If ten people join, it will support one child's total needs for one month."

In August, 2003, Tommy expressed his desire to build another leper colony near Chiang Mai, Thailand. He also marveled that the personal pediatrician of the Mongolian Prime Minister's children had resigned in order to serve full-time at the Gobi Desert hospital.

Over a year earlier, lepers in the Prapadange Leper Colony had asked Tommy with much hesitation and stammering whether he thought there could ever be a room built that was cool in the summer months. The steaming summers sometimes boasted temperatures of well over 100 degrees. Tommy could say that their dream had come true. There was now a large day-room where the lepers could gather. Private rooms were not air conditioned but things usually cooled off some during the night anyway. This air conditioning was the most comfortable environment the lepers had ever experienced.

In October, Tommy announced joyfully that Mitch had married dear Baljmaa, so now Tommy had a Thai daughter and a Mongolian daughter-in-law.

A month later, Mitch wrote that his new wife's mother, Oumaa, finally received Christ as her Savior following years of spiritual resistance.

Mitch asked for prayer for his language study and wrote of having so many children in Sunday meetings that he had to begin offering Children's Church on Saturdays too. Copies of a Mongolian children's Bible printed in Singapore had also arrived complete with striking color illustrations. Children loved the Bibles and now there was a daily Bible study for children in the Gobi desert with an attendance of at least twenty-five.

It's difficult to imagine, but one of the kindest leper workers at the Prapadange Leper Colony had been converted from a life of sickening brutality. As a policeman, he'd murdered 411 individuals. A small number of killings may have been justified, but in most cases, he admitted claiming unjustly that they tried to escape or attack him.

The Holy Spirit's movement and the response of individuals is truly beyond our comprehension. In October, according to records in Thailand and Mongolia only one person was saved. However, the following month, hundreds responded. Two Thai government officials and one military man were born again. In addition, 600 letters arrived from prisoners reporting that they had received Jesus. Tommy wasn't even aware that prisons had been receiving the radio broadcasts.

Tommy received a call for help from his adopted daughter, Young Suei. She and nine invalid friends had been living in a hospital in Chiang Mai. Buddhist officials had grown ugly, harshly demanding that they receive half of all that these ten invalids were receiving from Christians toward their hospital bills. Because the Christians felt this was unfair, they were being terribly mistreated.

Tommy rushed to Young Suei's aid and decided that the only lasting solution to this conflict was to transfer the group to the children's home in Chiang Rai. Tommy didn't have any idea how he could feed and house ten adults, but he prayed about it, and, days later, he received a check for $32,000.

As the year, 2003, came to an end, Tommy and Mitch felt very optimistic about progress in both Thailand and Mongolia. Churches were growing and a Thai camp meeting yielded seven converts.

Several Hill Tribe villages were transplanted; Tommy had found that buying land and making the villages self-sufficient with electricity and water helped prevent cults from luring them with food and trinkets.

The Thai leper colony now contained thirty-five lepers, there was a ministry to the deaf, and the children's home was again being expanded.

Bible college students were crossing the Mekong River into Laos and spreading the gospel there.

The hospital in the Gobi Desert now staffed three doctors, three nurses, two janitors, two cooks, two fire stokers, and a bookkeeper. The Gobi children's home housed thirty-five children.

The infant church in Mongolia had started out reaching only the very poor, outcasts, street people. But now the churches were beginning to fill with doctors, lawyers, teachers, and government officials. This was enabling the church to expand outreaches to the poor and disadvantaged.

Gobi children were presenting two different Christmas plays this year, and many nomads and others who would not yet attend a church would attend a play. It was an effective means of outreach.

Mitch also reported new access to a women's prison. This was remarkable because the old Communist system made it very difficult for religious groups to enter a prison.

With the dawn of 2004, Tommy reported an exciting problem. The ministries in Thailand and Mongolia were outgrowing the capacity of Tommy, Mitch, and other 'outsiders' to administrate. The policy for church planting had always been to train and ordain native pastors, then support a fledgling church to a point of independence. But now Tommy was deciding to turn the Thai children's homes completely over to Christian nationals to administrate. He claimed the verse Paul penned in 2 Corinthians 10:15b "Our hope is that, when your faith is increased that we shall be enlarged by you abundantly according to our rule, to preach the gospel in the regions beyond you...."

Trouble arose almost immediately for Mitch's ministry in the women's prison because of several prisoner escapes, but a long conference with the warden restored permission to come and minister twice per month. In one meeting, 140 inmates sat in a room with temperatures below zero to hear the gospel. This was no small thing. Over half of the women in Mongolian prisons are incarcerated for murdering their husbands. Tommy jokes that even though he was a Golden Gloves champ, he's never met a woman in Mongolia he thinks he could out-box. Once, he witnessed two women skillfully corner a horse; one then grabbed the horse around the neck, hoisted it, and wrestled it to the ground. Yet when these tough women heard the gospel, fifteen immediately responded to the salvation invitation.

The prison only supplied meals. Soap, shampoo, medicine, and other items had to be brought in by family or friends. But when prisoners were asked what the team could bring for them, every woman asked for only one thing, a Bible. One month after Bibles were supplied, the warden said she'd do all she could to give Mitch's team access to men's prisons also.

Tommy experienced a third minor heart attack in April and had to fly to the U.S. for assistance and for rest.

Most people in the Gobi Desert never had either the means or the opportunity to have any dental work done. A Christian dentist who offered her services reported treating 519 children and many adult nomads. All of these heard the gospel while they were there.

Mitch wrote home of the construction of a new church building. There's a touch of humor for us in a description that was surely far from humorous at the time: "If you have never built anything in a Third World country, you are really missing out on a big headache. Everything we know and have learned in the States about contracts, materials, hiring people, sub-contracting, and all other business matters are done completely opposite here."

However, one way in which construction was similar to the American experience was the fact that builders and sub-contractors constantly dragged their feet and missed deadlines.

In July, one of the greatest surprises was that the Mongolian women's prison warden accepted Christ. Forty-nine Mongolian women prisoners also committed their lives to Christ as Savior. They wanted to be baptized but were not permitted outside prison grounds under any circumstances. Amazingly, the prison warden allowed Tommy and Mitch to bring in a small rubber swimming pool, and there was joy and laughter as women stepped forward, one by one, to be dunked in the little pool. For this, the prison warden was relieved of her duties, but she simply joined Tommy's mission team.

August brought news of a new Thai preacher joining the ministry who would be preaching in twenty villages and many marketplaces each month.

The Mongolian children's home had grown from twenty children to forty. Technically, all of the children could not be considered orphans. What sometimes occurred was that a Gobi couple would bear a child, the man later might abandon the wife, and without the means to feed and care for the child, she'd forsake him or her at a church or police station.

A new church was being built in Ulaan Baatar, and this made a total of six churches in Mongolia counting the one in the Gobi Desert. Two hundred and fifty children now attended children's services.

Mitch and Baljmaa had also been witnessing for a long time to the manager of their apartment building and she was born again.

In September, the first evangelistic revival meetings ever were held at Mae Lao Leper Colony. Lepers who could barely walk, some crawling on hands and knees went to homes surrounding the colony and invited people to the services. Following the meetings, some lepers began going to surrounding villages with gospel tracts.

That fall, Mitch and Baljmaa were again reminded that their tallies of converts may be far from accurate. A 75-year-old man approached them after a church service and explained that four years before, as he passed the hospital, someone inside the fence anonymously passed a Bible to him. He went home, began reading, and within a few months read the book from Genesis to Revelation. He believed the book, believed in Jesus, and was saved by himself in his home.

Tommy told a somewhat similar story. They had distributed Chick gospel tracts throughout both Mongolia and Thailand. One Sunday an 85-year-old man appeared at a service claiming that he had found a gospel tract, read it, and done what it instructed. He told Tommy, "I feel different inside. Is there something wrong with me?"

"No," Tommy said, "you've just been born again."

The man wanted to tell everyone about it, and he immediately joined the church. A few days later he brought Tommy some Thai money and handed it to him. It was the equivalent of about one dollar.

The man said, "This is all I have. Use it in some of your good work."

As Mitch saw conversions such as this on every side, he wrote, "We can witness at every opportunity, let our light shine, pray for the lost, but only God convicts and saves."

In January, 2005, Tommy reported that he'd been feeling fatigued and somewhat listless. But he knew he needed to visit stations in the Gobi so he and a small party set out. About 200 miles later, one of the tires went flat. There is no convenient situation for a flat, but the 20 below zero temperatures didn't help. As they changed the tire, three nomads appeared and asked Tommy if he could tell them how to reach Heaven. He explained the gospel to them and they immediately received Christ.

Because it's so dangerous to drive without a spare in the desert, Tommy and his party had to return to Ulaan Baatar to buy a new spare. When they returned to the spot, they were able to give Bibles to the three new believers and quickly teach them some basic truth.

After driving a bit farther, the vehicle had another flat, but the group didn't care. Satan's attempt to discourage them had only allowed God to fulfill His intentions for the three new believers.

Occasionally God bestows rather unusual benefits upon His children. The most valuable gift anyone can give another in Mongolia is a horse. A government official, grateful for all Harbor Evangelism International had done for his nation, brought his prize race horse to Tommy and gave it to him as a gift. Tommy was grateful, but at age 72, with his heart history, he didn't think it best to begin training as a jockey at that time.

Another unusual honor occurred. Harbor Evangelism became known as the only mission agency in Mongolia who had won a pig farmer to Christ. Incidentally, this was the nation's *only* known pig farmer.

February is a national holiday in Mongolia, and therefore, as Mitch explained, they call it "white month". It's a celebration of their invaluable livestock and Mongolians can only eat things that are white.

Mitch also noted a matter for prayer. A Korean charismatic church about a mile from Mitch's church was spreading gossip to the effect that the church was actually a cultic Mormon church and that citizenry should stay away.

In March, for the first time, Tommy mentioned Mike and Heather Ivey as co-workers who had joined the team and who now served primarily among the invalids of Chiang Mai. He commended them as great servants and soul winners.

April's prayer letter from Mitch contained several creative ideas. To encourage believers to take the Discipleship class, upon their completion, Mitch decided to present them publically with a diploma. Pride shone on their faces as they each marched up to receive theirs.

Another idea Mitch was seeking to implement was making it possible for Christian families in the U.S. to adopt unwanted Mongolian babies.

Though many people were being reached, Mitch longed to reach more with the gospel. Then he began recognizing how many Mongolians long to learn English. He began to offer English classes and people were already flocking to the sessions. Being a good ole boy from the South, the only peculiarity Mitch began to notice was a lot of neighborhood Mongolians speaking English with a touch of Southern twang.

Tommy described Muslim violence that was increasing in three southern provinces in Thailand, and Muslims were threatening to spread the terrorism throughout the nation. A plea for intercession was sent out.

Tommy also requested prayer for the pastor serving at the Prapadange Leper Colony. At seventy-nine years of age, he was blinded by leprosy and his toes had been amputated, leaving his feet in very poor condition.

On the positive side, Tommy announced that out of the 250 individuals who had attended summer Bible camp, 98 were baptized in one day, and others also expressed interest in the Christian faith.

In Mitch's May prayer letter, he informed supporters of a new president in Mongolia who was making things more difficult for believers. The government would not give church permits to Christians and would not allow any church signs. Therefore, the only publicity possible was discreet word-of-mouth.

Larry Franklin, a missionary to children's teachers, arrived for ten days, and taught Mitch, Baljmaa and all their instructors ways to improve their teaching and their ministry to children.

In one of the children's churches in Ulaan Baatar, a girl of fifteen gave her heart to Christ. Soon afterward, she was discovered to have cancer of the lower intestine. Due to poor health care facilities in Mongolia, Mitch and Baljmaa took her by train to medical facilities in China. Sadly, doctors in China reported that the cancer was too advanced for successful removal. She was given only a few weeks to live.

No one else in the girl's family was saved, so every day Mitch and Baljmaa came to the home and prayed with her. For the next three weeks, they watched as her body quickly withered away. The day before her death, she smiled and told her family that she was excited to see Jesus.

The funeral service was held in the Ulaan Baatar church building. After the service, the family met with Mitch and said they wanted the joy the young girl had, and they wanted to be with her in Heaven some day. Her parents and a younger brother and sister prayed to receive Christ as Savior.

Several months later, Mitch reported a remarkable occurrence. Throughout the summer, he and Baljmaa had been jumping through governmental hoops, trying desperately to receive a permit so that their meetings would be considered legal. Every attempt failed, yet the pair continued to pray unceasingly. Then out of the blue, the government suddenly granted a blanket permit. This meant that, not only could they hold unimpeded meetings and have signs in front of their churches, but they could also hold public meetings anywhere in Mongolia.

Mitch and Baljmaa went wild. They began driving a flatbed trailer into public parks, and hooking up a small generator to speakers and musical instruments. They they'd blow up balloons and give out Popsicles to children, drawing a huge crowd, after which they sang and presented the gospel. Their only limitation was that only one month of temperate weather remained to allow such outreach.

The fall brought tremendous blessings as well as severe trials. Tommy and Jo Ann lost everything they owned in the U.S., including their home, in Hurricane Katrina. As they reeled from that catastrophe, word came that a faithful Mongolian church member had been beaten brutally by a Buddhist. Tommy was outraged.

He wrote, "There is not much to a man who beats up young girls. Please pray for this man."

On the positive side, God used a simple shower to help convince Gobi village leaders to request that churches be built in their towns. Tommy and Mitch had built showers in the Gobi hospital, and people had never experienced this easy way to stay clean. If having a shower attached to a church would help start a church in a new village, they figured 'why not'?

Also, a converted warden from the women's correctional facility in Mongolia decided to visit women's prisons in America to see how she could operate the institution more efficiently. When she returned, she wrote a book describing the things she learned. Mitch hoped that this warden and her book would be instrumental in opening opportunities in other Mongolian prisons.

Chapter Fourteen

Near the close of 2005, eight village chiefs from deep in the Gobi Desert sent a representative to Tommy with an urgent request. It should be understood that in a Communist nation such as Mongolia, a majority of citizens probably knew little to nothing about Buddhism, Islam, Hindiusm, or Christianity. In fact, these chiefs went first to the Buddhist headquarters pleading for them to come and teach them about God. They even offered to build a Buddhist temple. But, realizing how deep into the desert these villages lay, the Buddhists turned them down. The chiefs had heard that these folks called Christians had done some good things for their nation, so, next, they approached Tommy.

Tommy gave a resounding yes, and promised that he would do everything possible to get the gospel to them and to build churches among them.

In February, 2006, Mitch had a lot of good news to relate. The Ulaan Baatar mission hospital was voted the best business in the city. The church had grown so much that builders were doubling the size of the structure. He had just baptized sixteen individuals. Twenty made professions in another meeting led by Tommy.

Mixed in with all the positive events, Mitch also expressed concern about the political power grab in the highest echelons of political prominence. The current president had promised to rid the nation of foreign religions and influence, and he was not going quietly into that good night.

Mitch also mentioned a flu epidemic. Almost all of the children in the orphanage had the illness simultaneously, and the –25 degree weather did not help. He expressed sadness regarding the death of a two-month-old infant named Garid who was just not strong enough to fight off the illness. With a humble spirit, Mitch thanked God that the government unequivocally ruled it a natural death, and no one even hinted that the mission hospital might be responsible.

The following month, there was an update from both Thailand and Mongolia. In Thailand, the church at Mae Lao Christian leper colony had grown to an average of over thirty-five attenders, a large congregation as leper churches go. In addition, another church was being built in Mae Hong Son city in northeastern Thailand. For the first time, Tommy stated how difficult it had become to keep accurate numbers for interested prospects and new converts. Numbers for discipleship students was even challenging, given the fact that new volunteers were constantly stepping forward.

April was a great month of harvesting. The governor of the Gobi became a Christian, as well as his wife and son. In addition, the assistant governor was converted. A second hospital was being constructed in the Gobi. Two orphanages were in operation, one with fifty-one children. There were seven churches and a prison ministry that was reaching out to a number of penitentiaries. In addition, seven more villages were clamoring for a church building and pastor.

On a more personal level, a Buddhist monk became a Christian, and stood unashamed before the master and the other monks and resigned his position, proclaiming that he had determined to serve Jesus Christ and not Buddha. Another young man named Munhaa, a student at the Buddhist university in Ulaan Baatar, began attending Bible studies. After about a month and a half, he came to Mitch and Baljmaa asking how to become a Christian. The very next day he was converted, and dropped out of school. Mitch said, "These are the kind of drop-outs we don't mind seeing."

Meanwhile, in Thailand, besides the children's home and the leper colonies, 200 individuals per month were signing up for Bible correspondence courses.

The following month, prayer was requested for a woman named Ganna. She taught a children's Bible class and personally brought about fifty people to services every Sunday. She was having cancer surgery, and Baljmaa said, "It may sound selfish, but we really cannot afford to lose this woman."

In September, 2007, Mitch reported three infants admitted into the Ulaan Baatar orphanage under tragic circumstances. A girl was found by the river with vodka in her bottle. The staff gave her the name Anu, which was the name of a famous Mongolian queen. Another female infant was abandoned by her mother at a hospital. She had transmitted syphilis to the infant, but with prompt treatment, the child was expected to recover. A little boy was also found by a roadside. Gripped tightly in his hand was a 100tg coin (equivalent to about a dime in U.S.). He would not let go of the coin and kept saying softly in Mongolian, "My mommy left me. My mommy left me."

The mission had bought a printing press and a Christian named Jeff Kruchkow was there to train Mitch in the operation of it. However, Mitch was so incredibly busy, he didn't have a spare minute. Fortunately, two Mongolian boys volunteered to take the training and Jeff reported that they were learning quickly. This meant that soon the Mongolian mission center would have its own printing business and the staff was excited.

By November, 600 home Bible study courses were being mailed out in Thailand each month to Buddhists and believers of other faiths. Many were being saved and coming to the mother church at the Chiang Mai children's home to be baptized.

Then in December, Tommy again visited Mongolia and, through his witness, eight Mongolian women were converted. It is much easier to influence the pliable hearts of children than Communist-hardened hearts of adults, so this was a great source of joy. When the women learned of baptism, they immediately wanted to be baptized. At that time, the weather was 20 below zero and Tommy mentioned that it would be more comfortable for them if they waited for warmer weather. But the women were adamant, so Tommy rented a building and tried to prepare some water that wasn't layered with ice. The women's faces beamed as they emerged from the water, cold but ecstatic.

Because of the fourteen stents in his heart arteries, Tommy must come back to America at least every four months. Since his many open heart surgeries, the doctors do not want him in a Third World hospital if something should go wrong.

Some may wonder, why does Tommy Tillman continue serving the Lord and expanding the ministries when his heart could simply stop beating at any moment? The answer may perhaps be understood, at least in part, through an illustration Tommy once heard from a sheep farmer. The farmer took him out to the farm and, as they watched hundreds of sheep grazing, the man said, "I always wondered why Jesus was described as a lamb led to the slaughter. Then we had our first sheep slaughter and I was amazed that when we slit their necks, they don't struggle, squeal, or fight back like pigs or goats. They lock their legs and stand quietly as their life's blood spills out. Then they fall forward and die. With a Savior like the Lamb of God, Tommy cannot stop preaching His gospel.

Another of Tommy's chief motivations is drawn from one of his hundreds of prayer letters. He writes:

"I fear for any work or church that no longer wants to grow and expand for our Lord."

One of the rare gifts both Tommy and Mitch possess is their simple manner of calling for more workers. For example, in a 2006 prayer letter, Mitch wrote from Mongolia: "The director of a prison with six hundred prisoners has offered anyone who would teach English to his prisoners and staff a free apartment and salary for one year. This apartment is in a town of 30,000 people about ten miles from the prison. It is a great opportunity for someone wanting to reach many for Christ..."

Though there would surely be some culture shock, some deprivations, some language study, and such, Mitch cuts right to the chase—to the incredible spiritual treasure and joy one could accrue, even for a commitment of only one year.

Tommy has now been preaching for about fifty years. Sometimes people tell him, "Missionaries like you will be at the very front of the line to receive rewards in heaven!"

"But I don't really believe that," Tommy says. "I think that churches who care for, pray, and give to missions throughout the world will perhaps be first because none of us could go out to these nations without that support, prayer, and love."

Another of Tommy's deeply felt convictions is that the entire world is a mission field and, in that sense, he is not to be placed on a pedestal. He sees the United States as one of the most crucial mission fields on earth. Through the decades he has seen many churches drifting away from the true gospel of Jesus Christ...allowing sin to infiltrate the congregation and "getting used to the darkness" that surrounds on every side.

We sometimes hear messages on the seven churches of Asia described in the book of Revelation: Ephesus, Smyrna, Pergamos, Thyatira, Sardis, Philadelphia, and Laodicea. Tommy believes that many churches in America in our day are similar in a big way to the Laodicean church: lukewarm, smugly self-satisfied, and blind to their true state.

If you meet Tommy Tillman, one of the first things you will notice is his down home sense of humor. He jokes, laughs easily, and cuts up like a schoolboy at times. But one matter he will never ever joke about is the Word of God and the work of God. And that is what is most remarkable about this simple man of God. He loves his God supremely and he reflects that love with a devotion to the Word of God and a compassion for people. This is what Tommy Tillman is about.

Tommy admits that Thailand and Mongolia comprise his real home. As a yonng man he read of how David Livingstone loved the Africans so much that when he died, he instructed that his heart be buried in Africa. Without a hint of melodrama, Tommy has talked to one of the mission doctors in Thailand and the doctor has agreed. When Tommy passes on, his heart will be removed and buried in his beloved Thailand. It's only symbolic of love, of course, for without God's love, Tommy Tillman would never have devoted his life to being a servant ambassador to thousands.

Epilogue

B elow is a list of what God has done in Thailand and Mongolia as of 2008. Soon this update regarding Harbor Evangelism International will be out of date, but of course, that's a blessing, because it shows that God is constantly expanding this ministry in many different directions. This book is only the beginning of a story that will not end until Christ bursts through the clouds to claim His own.

Twenty-nine Years in Thailand

1) Leper colony in Mae Lao, Thailand with church built on premises.
2) Orphanage right outside Chiang Mai. Church built on premises.
3) Invalid home right outside Chiang Mai. Church on premises.
4) Hill Tribe Church in Mae Hong Song in northwest Thailand.

5) Two leper churches in southern part of Thailand.

6) Leper church at Prapadange Leper Colony, just outside Bangkok.

7) Over six hundred home Bible courses being mailed out each month primarily to Buddhist believers. Many have been converted and even come to the church at the children's home to be baptized. They also receive a diploma upon the completion of the course.

8) Many churches planted which are now indigenous.

Twelve Years in Mongolia

1) Mother church for adults in Ulaan Baatar, capitol city of Mongolia.

2) Church for adults on the outskirts of Ulaan Baatar.

3) Nine children's churches spread out all over Ulaan Baatar. Meetings are typically on Saturdays.

4) Three churches in the Gobi Desert with eight still to be built.

5) Prison ministry with church building inside the women's prison.

6) Orphanage with twelve children at this writing. This orphanage placed children up for adoption.

7) Printing ministry: printing Bibles and gospel tracts.

8) English lessons taught in university. Gospel is given out at these classes.
9) Translation ministry.
10) Ministry with street people.
11) Two hospitals built and a third in process. Christian doctors and nurses serve in these hospitals.

ABOUT THE AUTHOR

Steve Fortosis earned a Ph.D. from Talbot School of Theology in La Mirada, California in 1990. He has taught on the college and seminary levels, and has written or co-written seven books and numerous articles. He lives in North Port, Florida and he and his wife, Debra, are members of Liberty Baptist Church of Sarasota. Under the leadership of Dr. Gary Jackson, the church considers it an honor to have helped support Tommy and Jo Ann Tillman's ministry for many years.

We are grateful to Jill Thomas, Liberty Baptist secretary, for electronically preparing the photos and captions in this book for submission to the publisher.

Printed in the United States
202218BV00001B/217-1524/P